101 Things To Do With Tofu

101 Things To Do With Tofu

BY
DONNA KELLY AND
ANNE TEGTMEIER

GIBBS SMITH
TO ENRICH AND INSPIRE HUMANKIND

24 23 22 21 20   5 4 3 2 1

Published by
Gibbs Smith
P.O. Box 667
Layton, Utah 84041

1.800.835.4993 orders
www.gibbs-smith.com

Printed and bound in Korea
Gibbs Smith books are printed on either recycled, 100% post-consumer
waste, FSC-certified papers or on paper produced from sustainable PEFC-
certified forest/controlled wood source. Learn more at www.pefc.org.

Library of Congress Cataloging-in-Publication Data

Names: Kelly, Donna, 1955- author. | Tegtmeier, Anne, author.
Title: 101 things to do with tofu / Donna Kelly, Anne Tegtmeier.
Other titles: One hundred one things to do with tofu
Description: First edition. | Layton, Utah : Gibbs Smith, Publisher, [2020] Identifiers:
LCCN 2019033511 | ISBN 9781423654537 (spiral bound) | ISBN 9781423612261 (epub)
Subjects: LCSH: Cooking (Tofu) | LCGFT: Cookbooks.
Classification: LCC TX814.5.T63 K45 2020 | DDC 641.6/5655--dc23
LC record available at https://lccn.loc.gov/2019033511

The authors dedicate this book to their
families, to their reader's families,
and to the many sweet serendipities and
rediscovered joys in life.

Many thanks to my trusty taste testers,
especially Tom, Patty, and TMA. I am
indebted to Faith and Amy for their
long-distance love, to the Tegtmeiers for
their support, and above all to Donna,
without whom I would not be here at
all, let alone embarking on yet another
adventure with her. I am truly grateful.
—A.C.T.

With gratitude to my co-author, Anne,
who is also my daughter, my friend, and
my culinary muse. May our adventures
be many, our sorrows be few and
our joys eternal. —D.M.K.

CONTENTS

Helpful Hints 9

Appetizers

Hot Spinach & Artichoke Dip 12 ● *Layered Goat Cheese Torte 13* ● *Vegan Pizza Bites 14* ● *Tofu Hummus 15* ● *Veggie Potstickers 16* ● *Savory Seasonings Cheesecake 17* ● *Sun-Dried Tomato Spread 18* ● *Pesto-Stuffed Mushrooms 19* ● *Sesame Soy Squares 20* ● *Vegetarian Pate 21*

Sauces, Dressings & Spreads

Tofu Mayonnaise 24 ● *Caesar Salad Dressing 25* ● *Cucumber Dill Dressing 26* ● *Easy Creamy Italian Dressing 27* ● *Easy Ranch Dressing 28* ● *Alfredo Sauce 29* ● *Tangy Thai Peanut Dip 30* ● *Healthy Hollandaise Sauce 31*

Soups & Salads

Tomato Onion Chowder 34 ● *Hot & Sour Soup 35* ● *Broccoli Cheddar Soup 36* ● *African Peanut Soup 37* ● *Ultimate Veggie Chili 38* ● *Vegetarian Goulash 39* ● *Vegan Gumbo 40* ● *Creamy Mushroom Soup 41* ● *Butternut Squash Soup 42* ● *Waldorf Salad 43* ● *Broccoli Madness Salad 44* ● *Layered Fiesta Chopped Salad 45* ● *Mock Chicken Salad 46* ● *Eggless Salad 47* ● *Creamy Pasta Salad 48*

Breakfast

Simple Tofu Scramble 50 ● *Breakfast Burritos 51* ● *Confetti Hash Brown Casserole 52* ● *Upside-Down Skillet Cake 53* ● *Tex-Mex Migas 54* ● *Any Fruit Quick Bread 55* ● *Smoothies 56* ● *Apple Streusel Coffee Cake 57* ● *Tofu Benedict 58* ● *Mix 'n' Match Muffins 59* ● *Vegan French Toast 60*

Kids' Favorites

Healthy Mac 'n' Cheese 62 ● Tofu Toes 63 ● Tofu Sloppy Joes 64 ●
Nutterballs 65 ● Fluffy Peanut Butter Spread 66 ● Hi-Pro-Tatoes 67 ●
Snack Parfaits 68

Main Dishes

Tofu Filets 70 ● Ground Tofu Filling 71 ● Homemade Veggie Burgers 72 ●
Three-Cheese Stuffed Shells 73 ● Tricolor Quiche 74 ● Cheese Fondue 75
● Festive Crescent Wreath 76 ● Veggie Calzone 77 ● Mushroom
Strudel 78 ● Roasted Vegetable Layered Casserole 79 ● Italian-Style
"Meat Loaf" 80 ● Veggie Stir-Fry 81 ● Tofu Mini Potpies 82
● Vegetarian Shepherd's Pie 83 ● Tofu Tamale Pie 84 ● Tofu Stroganoff 85
● Sublime Spinach Lasagna 86 ● Tofu Parmigiana 87 ● Tofu
Sandwiches 88 ● Chicken-Fried Tofu Triangles 90 ● Cheatballs 91

International Entrees

Thai Coconut Curry 94 ● Tofu Tikka Masala 95 ● Spanakopita Triangles 96
● Tofu Piccata 97 ● Sweet & Sour Soy 98 ● Tofu Fried Rice 99 ●
Stromboli Roll 100 ● Vegan Palak Paneer 101 ● Vegetarian Paella 102 ●
Black Bean Enchiladas 103 ● Tofu Cacciatore 104 ●
Vegetarian Pad Thai 105

Desserts

Tripleberry Tarts 108 ● Rebirth by Chocolate 109 ● Raspberry Chocolate
Chunk Pie 110 ● Gooey Spice Bars 111 ● Peanut Butter Cup 112 ● Creamy
Cookie Pie 113 ● Raspberry Delight 114 ● Tofu Pumpkin Pie 115 ●
Dairy-Free Chocolate Pudding 116 ● Classic Cheesefake 117 ● Chocolate
Cheesefake 118 ● Lemon Custard Cups 119 ● Coconut Almond Bars
120 ● Creme Brulee 121 ● Tofu Ice Cream Desserts 122 ● Lemon
Raspberry Tiramisu 123 ● World's Healthiest Brownies 124 ●
Dessert Pizza 125

HELPFUL HINTS

1. What is tofu? It is soybean curd. Tofu is to soy milk as cottage cheese is to cow's milk. The resulting product is a nutritious and versatile food, suitable for vegans, vegetarians, and those who simply want to reap the benefits of including more soy products in their diets. Its neutral flavor adapts easily to any kind of recipe, from the most savory entrees to the sweetest desserts.

2. Basic nutritional information: Soy is an easily digestible form of protein, and is a complete protein food source (other plant sources of protein must be combined with other foods to form a complete chain of amino acids, i.e. beans and rice). The amount of protein in tofu varies according to variety—the firmer the variety, the higher the protein content. Other health benefits of soy include calcium, iron, B vitamins and naturally occurring phytoestrogens. Tofu is one of the least processed forms of soy. It has no cholesterol and is low in calories and saturated fat.

3. Tofu comes in four basic varieties: extra-firm, firm, soft, and silken (not to be confused with soft). Firm is the most commonly available and widely used. The most popular brands, and the ones that are used in these recipes, come packaged in water. Some brands come packaged in smaller, airtight cartons. There are also "lite" versions of each variety that are even lower in fat and calories; feel free to use them in these recipes.

4. With the exception of silken tofu, which generally comes in 16-ounce packages, make sure you account for the amount of water in each package. The total weight of a package of firm tofu in water might be 16 ounces, for example, but the net weight of the tofu itself would be 14 ounces.

5. Some types of tofu may be substituted with another. If extra-firm is not available, then firm may be used; if soft is not available, silken may be used. However, do not substitute extra-firm for other varieties.

6. Most supermarkets now carry tofu in their produce sections, while natural and specialty grocery stores may carry it in or near the dairy cases.

7. Some tofu is available already marinated, smoked or otherwise pre-seasoned; all recipes in this book are based on plain-flavored tofu, but feel free to experiment with flavored varieties!

8. Many recipes call for tofu that has been frozen and then thawed. This changes the texture of the tofu, making it chewier and easy to crumble. When frozen, the moisture in the tofu separates from the bean curd, making it easier to squeeze out excess water. The tofu becomes spongy and porous, ideal for absorbing flavors. Tofu can be frozen in its own water or drained and wrapped in plastic until ready to use. Tofu can also be cut into slabs or cubes before freezing, or it can be frozen whole.

9. For unopened containers of tofu, check the manufacturer's use-by date. Once opened, leftover tofu can be refrigerated for up to a week. Just cover it in water and then change the water daily.

10. Recipes commonly call for tofu to be drained and/or pressed. To drain it, simply pour off the water. To press it, a number of techniques can be used. One method calls for wrapping the tofu in paper or cloth dish towels, then setting something heavy on top of it (like a large glass jar). Another method is to sandwich it between two plates and gently press, pouring off the water. If a recipe calls for the tofu to be crumbled, you can wrap it in clean dish towels and wring the towels out, both squeezing out the moisture and crumbling the block of tofu.

11. If using tofu in an uncooked recipe, we recommend cutting the block of tofu into 4 pieces and boiling for 5 minutes. This improves the overall taste and texture of the tofu.

12. We tried to include only items that are easily found at any supermarket. Unfamiliar spices are usually found in the international foods aisle. Tempeh and seitan are other meat substitutes: tempeh is related to tofu in that it is a fermented soy product, while seitan is formed from wheat gluten. These are usually found in the produce department, along with tofu itself.

APPETIZERS

HOT SPINACH & ARTICHOKE DIP

8 ounces	**silken tofu**
1 tablespoon	**lemon juice**
1 package (8 ounces)	**cream cheese,** softened
1 box (10 ounces)	**frozen chopped spinach,** thawed and drained
1 jar (7.5 ounces)	**marinated artichoke hearts,** drained and chopped
1 cup	**grated mozzarella cheese**
1/2 cup	**grated Parmesan cheese**

Preheat oven to 350 degrees.

Blend tofu with lemon juice and cream cheese in a food processor or blender until smooth. Mix in remaining ingredients, stirring with a spoon. Sprinkle additional Parmesan cheese on top as a garnish, if desired. Bake in an 8-inch pie pan for 50–60 minutes, or until bubbly and browned. Let cool slightly and serve warm with bagel crisps, pita chips or thin slices of toasted French bread. Makes 4–6 servings.

LAYERED GOAT CHEESE TORTE

16 ounces	**goat cheese,** divided
14 ounces	**firm tofu,** drained and divided
1 teaspoon	**garlic powder**
1 teaspoon	**salt,** divided
1 jar (8 ounces)	**pesto sauce**
1 jar (12 ounces)	**sun-dried tomatoes in oil**

Generously coat an 8-inch round cake pan or springform pan with nonstick cooking spray.

In a food processor, blend 10 ounces goat cheese, 10 ounces tofu, garlic powder and $1/2$ teaspoon salt. Spread in pan. Press excess oil from pesto sauce and spread on top of goat cheese mixture.

In food processor, blend remaining goat cheese, tofu, salt, and the sun-dried tomatoes and oil. Carefully spread the tomato mixture on top. Chill for at least 1 hour, or until firm. Invert onto a plate. Serve with bagel crisps or thin slices of toasted French bread. Makes 4–6 servings.

VEGAN PIZZA BITES

1 loaf	**French bread,** about 2 inches in diameter
4 tablespoons	**olive oil,** divided
14 ounces	**firm tofu,** drained
1 tablespoon	**soy sauce**
4 tablespoons	**tomato paste**
1 teaspoon each	**dried basil, oregano and thyme**
1 clove	**garlic,** minced
$^1/_4$ teaspoon	**cayenne pepper**
	salt and black pepper, to taste
$^1/_4$ cup	**grated soy Parmesan cheese** (optional)

Preheat oven to 450 degrees.

Slice bread into $^1/_2$-inch-thick rounds and place on a dry baking sheet. Brush slices with 1–2 tablespoons olive oil. Blend remaining olive oil and other ingredients except cheese in a food processor or blender until a smooth paste forms. Spread the mixture over the bread slices. Bake until bread is golden and toasted, about 15 minutes. If using cheese, sprinkle on after the first 5 minutes. Makes 24 bites.

TOFU HUMMUS

14 ounces	**firm tofu,** drained
1 can (15 ounces)	**garbanzo beans,** drained and rinsed
1 clove	**garlic,** chopped
1 tablespoon	**sesame oil**
$1/2$ teaspoon	**salt,** or more to taste
2 tablespoons	**lemon juice**

Blend all ingredients in a food processor or blender until smooth.
Serve at room temperature or slightly chilled. Serve with large crackers,
toasted pita triangles or bagel crisps. Makes 6–8 servings.

VARIATION: For a chunkier style hummus, smash all ingredients together with a potato masher instead of processing in a food processor or
blender.

VEGGIE POTSTICKERS

3 cups	**shredded cabbage,** mixed with 1 teaspoon salt
14 ounces	**extra-firm tofu,** frozen and thawed,
	then drained and crumbled
4	**scallions,** finely chopped
2 cloves	**garlic,** minced
1 tablespoon	**grated ginger**
1 1/2 tablespoons	**soy sauce**
2	**egg whites,** gently beaten with fork
24	**wonton wrappers**
2 tablespoons	**oil,** divided

Let cabbage and salt mixture sit 30 minutes in a colander in a sink. Press the cabbage down to squeeze out any excess moisture and then transfer to a mixing bowl. Combine with crumbled tofu, scallions, garlic, ginger, soy sauce and egg whites. Cover and refrigerate for at least 1 hour. Lay wonton wrappers out on a flat surface. Put a heaping tablespoon of filling in the center of each and then moisten the outer edges with water. Fold the square in half to create a triangle and seal.

When half the wrappers are filled, heat 1 tablespoon oil in a nonstick frying pan with lid. Lay the potstickers in the pan and cook, uncovered, over medium-high heat about 5 minutes, or until golden on the bottom. Add about 1/2 cup water to the pan, reduce heat to low and cover. Cook about 10 minutes, or until most of the water is absorbed. Remove cover and increase heat back to medium-high; cook an additional 4 minutes. Transfer finished potstickers to paper towels and repeat the process until all the filling has been used. Makes 24 potstickers.

SAVORY SEASONINGS CHEESECAKE

8 ounces	**silken tofu**
3 packages (8 ounces each)	**regular or soy cream cheese,** softened
2 tablespoons	**lemon juice**
3 tablespoons	**flour**
4	**shallots,** minced
2 cloves	**garlic,** minced
2 teaspoons	**Italian Seasoning**
$1/4$ teaspoon	**dried tarragon**
	salt and pepper, to taste
zest of 1	**lemon**
$1/4$ cup each	**fresh minced parsley, grated zucchini and grated carrot**
$1^1/4$ cups	**breadcrumbs**

Preheat oven to 400 degrees.

Process tofu, cream cheese, and lemon juice in a food processor until smooth. Add flour, shallots, garlic, seasonings and lemon zest and then process until incorporated. Stir in parsley, zucchini and carrot. Spray a springform pan with cooking spray and sprinkle breadcrumbs over the bottom. Pour cheesecake mixture into pan and bake 15 minutes. Reduce heat to 325 degrees and cook 50 minutes more, or until top is medium brown. Let cool completely (or chill overnight) before serving. Serve in small slices or spread over crackers. Makes 8 servings.

VARIATION: Garnish with basil leaves and tomato roses.

SUN-DRIED TOMATO SPREAD

16 ounces **firm tofu,** drained and pressed
1 jar (16 ounces) **sun-dried tomatoes in oil,** undrained
2 teaspoons **garlic salt**

Blend all ingredients in a food processor or blender until fully blended. Chill 1 hour or overnight. Serve with large crackers, bagel crisps or thin slices of toasted French bread. Keeps in refrigerator up to 1 week. Makes 8–10 servings.

PESTO-STUFFED MUSHROOMS

7 ounces	**firm tofu,** drained
3 tablespoons	**pesto sauce**
2 cups	**seasoned dry breadcrumbs**
$1/2$ cup	**grated Parmesan cheese**
24	**medium-size brown button mushrooms,** stems removed
$1/4$ cup	**canola oil**
$1/2$ cup	**finely grated mozzarella cheese**

Preheat oven to 350 degrees.

In a medium-size mixing bowl, mash tofu with a fork until finely crumbled. Mix in pesto sauce, breadcrumbs and Parmesan cheese. Brush mushroom caps with oil and place on a baking sheet. Fill caps with tofu mixture, mounding and rounding mixture on each cap. Bake 25–30 minutes, or until cooked through and lightly browned. Remove from oven and sprinkle with mozzarella cheese. Makes 24 appetizers.

SESAME SOY SQUARES

2 tablespoons	**sesame oil**
1/4 cup	**soy sauce**
1/4 cup	**rice vinegar**
1/2 tablespoon	**brown sugar**
1 teaspoon	**crushed red pepper flakes**
juice of 1	**lime**
1 teaspoon	**cornstarch**
14 ounces	**extra-firm tofu,** frozen, thawed and cut into 1/4-inch squares
1/4 cup	**peanut oil**
1/2 cup	**toasted sesame seeds**
2 tablespoons	**chopped fresh cilantro**

Whisk together first seven ingredients. Pour half the mixture into a 9 x 13-inch baking dish and then lay the tofu in the marinade. Pour remaining marinade over the top. Cover and chill for at least 1 hour.

Heat peanut oil in a frying pan. Add tofu squares, reserving any excess marinade, about 5 or 6 pieces at a time. Saute until light brown and starting to crisp (about 3 minutes on each side). Add the reserved marinade to the pan and cook until syrupy and bubbly, or reduced by half. Sprinkle sesame seeds and cilantro over squares when finished. Serve on top of your favorite crackers. Makes 8–10 servings.

VEGETARIAN PATE

14 ounces	**firm tofu,** drained and pressed
2 tablespoons	**liquid smoke**
2 tablespoons	**olive oil**
1	**large onion,** chopped
2 cloves	**garlic,** chopped
4 cups	**sliced portobello, porcini and/or shiitake mushrooms**
2 tablespoons	**white wine or white wine vinegar**
1 teaspoon	**dried thyme**
$^1/_2$ teaspoon each	**salt and coarse black pepper**
$^1/_4$ teaspoon	**chipotle chili powder**
$^1/_2$ cup	**cashews**
2 tablespoons	**flour**
2 tablespoons	**chopped fresh parsley**

Cut tofu into 2-inch slabs and then soak in liquid smoke in a shallow, covered bowl at least 3 hours. Preheat oven to 350 degrees and spray a loaf pan with nonstick spray. Heat oil in a large frying pan and saute onion and garlic over medium heat until softened, about 4–5 minutes. Add mushrooms, vinegar, and seasonings and cook 5 minutes more, or until moisture has evaporated; remove from heat. Grind nuts in a food processor until a fine meal forms. Add flour and parsley, pulsing until integrated. Add mushroom mixture and tofu, discarding excess marinade, and process until uniform and mostly smooth. Transfer to loaf pan and bake for 45 minutes. Cool completely before chilling, then cover and refrigerate at least 3–4 hours before serving. Invert the loaf pan, using a plate or serving platter, and serve with crackers. Makes about 24 servings.

SAUCES, DRESSINGS & SPREADS

TOFU MAYONNAISE

8 ounces	**firm tofu,** drained
2 tablespoons	**canola oil**
2 tablespoons	**lemon juice**
1 teaspoon	**dry mustard**
$1/2$ teaspoon	**salt**

Blend all ingredients together in a blender until smooth. Keep refrigerated in an airtight container for up to 1 week. Makes about 1 $1/4$ cups.

GARLIC VARIATION: Add 1 teaspoon minced garlic or more to taste while blending.

SOUTHWEST VARIATION: Add 1 teaspoon chipotle chili powder or more to taste while blending.

PESTO VARIATION: Add 1 teaspoon pesto or more to taste while blending.

CAESAR SALAD DRESSING

1/4 cup	**grated fresh Parmesan cheese**
4 cloves	**garlic,** crushed
2 tablespoons	**red wine vinegar**
1 1/2 tablespoons	**Worcestershire sauce**
2 tablespoons	**Dijon mustard**
16 ounces	**silken tofu**
1/4 cup	**olive oil**
1/2 teaspoon each	**salt and coarse black pepper**

Pulse cheese and garlic in a food processor or blender. Add vinegar,
Worcestershire and mustard; blend until combined. Add tofu, oil,
salt and pepper; blend until smooth. More oil may be added to adjust
consistency. Refrigerate in an airtight container for up to 2 weeks.
Makes about 2 1/2 cups.

CUCUMBER DILL DRESSING

1 **large cucumber,** peeled and seeded
8 ounces **silken tofu**
1/4 cup **white wine vinegar**
1/4 cup **fresh dill,** or more to taste
1 teaspoon **salt**

Cut cucumber into chunks. Combine all ingredients in a food processor or high-speed blender until smooth. Chill until ready to serve. Refrigerate in an airtight container for up to 2 weeks. Makes about 2 1/2 cups.

EASY CREAMY ITALIAN DRESSING

8 ounces	**silken tofu**
$^1/_2$ cup	**olive oil**
$^1/_4$ cup	**red wine vinegar**
1 package (0.75 ounce)	**Italian seasoning mix**

Combine all ingredients in a food processor or high-speed blender until smooth. Chill until ready to serve. Refrigerate in an airtight container for up to 2 weeks. Makes about 2 cups.

EASY RANCH DRESSING

14 ounces	**firm tofu**
3/4 cup	**olive oil**
1/2 cup	**white wine vinegar**
1 package (0.75 ounce)	**ranch seasoning mix**
1 teaspoon	**coarsely ground black pepper,**
	or more to taste

Combine all ingredients in a food processor or high-speed blender until smooth. Chill until ready to serve. Refrigerate in an airtight container for up to 2 weeks. Makes about 2 1/2 cups.

VARIATION: For Parmesan Peppercorn dressing, add 1/2 cup grated Parmesan cheese or cheese substitute and an additional tablespoon of coarse black pepper.

ALFREDO SAUCE

16 ounces	**silken tofu**
2 cloves	**garlic,** chopped
2 tablespoons	**olive oil**
1 teaspoon	**dried parsley**
$^1/_2$ teaspoon each	**salt and coarsely ground pepper**
$^1/_2$ cup	**grated Parmesan cheese**

Puree all ingredients except cheese in food processor or blender. Transfer to saucepan and heat over medium-high heat. Stir in cheese and then cook until melted. Serve over your favorite pasta. Makes about 2$^1/_2$ cups.

VARIATION: For Pesto Alfredo, add $^1/_4$ cup fresh basil and 2 tablespoons finely ground pine nuts or 3 tablespoons prepared pesto sauce to mixture in blender.

TANGY THAI PEANUT DIP

1 1/2 cups	**chunky peanut butter**
16 ounces	**silken tofu**
2 tablespoons	**malt or cider vinegar**
2 tablespoons	**soy sauce**
2 tablespoons	**grated gingerroot**
2 cloves	**garlic,** minced
3 tablespoons	**minced fresh cilantro**
1 teaspoon	**salt**
1 teaspoon	**cayenne pepper,** or more to taste
3 tablespoons	**lime juice**
1/4 cup	**hot water**

Combine all ingredients in a food processor or blender, adding the
1/4 cup hot water just before blending. Puree until well-combined but
a little bit chunky; add extra water to reach desired consistency if too
thick. Chill until ready to serve. Serve with cucumber slices, carrot
sticks and other raw vegetables. Makes about 3 1/4 cups.

VARIATION: Add 2 tablespoons sugar (especially recommended if using
natural, unsweetened peanut butter) and top with finely chopped
peanuts and more minced fresh cilantro.

HEALTHY HOLLANDAISE SAUCE

16 ounces	**silken tofu**
$^1/_2$ cup	**olive oil**
1 tablespoon	**sugar**
2 tablespoons	**lemon juice**
2 tablespoons	**butter-flavored granules**
1 teaspoon	**salt** (optional)

Blend all ingredients together in a food processor or blender until smooth. Heat in microwave on medium heat until very warm, but not hot, about 60–90 seconds. Serve over broccoli, asparagus spears, cauliflower or Eggs Benedict. Refrigerate in an airtight container for up to 1 week. Makes $2^1/_2$ cups.

SOUPS & SALADS

TOMATO ONION CHOWDER

1	**large yellow onion,** diced
6 tablespoons	**butter or margarine**
2 tablespoons	**minced garlic**
1 cup	**minced fresh basil leaves**
2 cans (28 ounces each)	**crushed tomatoes in puree**
2 cups	**vegetable broth**
16 ounces	**silken tofu**
	salt, to taste

In a large stockpot, saute onion in butter until translucent. Add garlic and saute another 2–3 minutes. Add basil and tomatoes. In a blender, blend broth and tofu. Add to soup mixture and then simmer for 20–30 minutes, stirring frequently. Add salt to taste and serve. Makes 6–8 servings.

VARIATION: For a smooth and creamy version, add onion, garlic and tomato to blender with the tofu and broth. Return to pot and add basil, continue as directed.

HOT & SOUR SOUP

I tablespoon	**cornstarch**
6 cups	**vegetable broth,** divided
I	**egg,** beaten
$^1/_4$ cup	**soy sauce**
I cup	**julienned shiitake or brown mushrooms**
I can (5 ounces)	**bamboo shoots,** drained and julienned
7 ounces	**firm tofu,** cut into small cubes
I teaspoon	**sesame oil**
I tablespoon each	**balsamic and red wine vinegars**
I teaspoon	**ground white pepper**
3	**green onions,** thinly sliced

Combine cornstarch and 2 tablespoons broth in a small bowl. Stir in egg with a fork and set aside.

In a medium saucepan, bring remaining broth, soy sauce, mushrooms and bamboo shoots to a boil; simmer 5 minutes. Add tofu and then stir in oil, vinegars and pepper and cook 3–5 minutes more. Remove pan from heat and drizzle in the egg mixture. Let sit for a minute to set. Return pan to heat and simmer a few minutes more, stirring constantly. Serve with green onions sprinkled on top. Makes 6 servings.

BROCCOLI CHEDDAR SOUP

8 cups	**chopped broccoli**
4 cups	**vegetable broth**
16 ounces	**silken tofu**
$^1/_2$ teaspoon	**nutmeg** (optional)
16 ounces	**sharp cheddar cheese,** grated
	salt, to taste

In a large pot, simmer broccoli in broth for 5–8 minutes, or until slightly softened but not mushy. Drain broth into a food processor or blender and add tofu and nutmeg, if desired; blend until smooth. Mash broccoli with potato masher in pot until a thick puree forms. Pour tofu mixture into pot and return to a simmer. Add cheese by the handful. Add salt to taste and serve warm. Makes 6–8 servings.

VARIATION: Replace broccoli with equal amount of cauliflower.

AFRICAN PEANUT SOUP

2 tablespoons	**olive oil**
$^1/_2$	**red bell pepper,** diced
1	**yellow onion,** diced
1 tablespoon	**minced garlic**
1 tablespoon	**minced cilantro**
2 cans (14 ounces each)	**vegetable broth**
16 ounces	**silken tofu**
1 can (15 ounces)	**crushed tomatoes in puree**
$^1/_2$ cup	**uncooked rice**
1 cup	**chunky peanut butter**
	chopped peanuts (optional)

Heat the oil over medium-high heat in a large stockpot. Saute bell pepper and onion until limp, about 2–3 minutes. Add garlic and cilantro and saute another minute. Blend broth and tofu in a blender or food processor until smooth. Pour into pot and then stir in tomatoes. Stir in rice and reduce heat to medium-low. Simmer gently for about 20 minutes, or until rice is done, stirring occasionally so rice will not stick to bottom of pan. Turn off heat and then stir in peanut butter until melted. (Taste to see if soup needs salt. The salt content of each brand of peanut butter varies.) Serve with additional chopped peanuts sprinkled on top, if desired. Makes 4–6 servings.

ASIAN VARIATION: Omit the crushed tomatoes and add 1 can (14 ounces) coconut milk.

ULTIMATE VEGGIE CHILI

1	**yellow onion,** chopped
1	**red bell pepper,** chopped
3 cloves	**garlic,** minced
2 tablespoons	**olive oil**
2 teaspoons	**cumin**
1 teaspoon each	**chili powder and red pepper flakes**
14 ounces	**extra-firm tofu,** frozen and thawed
2 cans (14 ounces each)	**diced tomatoes,** undrained
1 can (28 ounces)	**crushed tomatoes,** undrained
2 cans (14 ounces each)	**black beans,** drained and rinsed
1 can (14 ounces)	**dark kidney beans,** drained and rinsed
1/2 cup	**frozen corn**
1/2 cup	**whole roasted cashews**
	salt and black pepper

In a large stockpot, saute onion, bell pepper and garlic in the olive oil over medium-high heat until onion starts to soften. Stir in spices. Crumble the thawed tofu into the mixture and saute 5 minutes more. Reduce heat to medium. Add tomatoes, black beans, kidney beans, corn and cashews; mix well. Reduce heat to low and simmer for 1 hour, stirring occasionally. Garnish with additional cashews, if desired. Add salt and pepper to taste. Makes 8 servings.

VARIATION: For a spicier, smokier version, add 1/2 teaspoon chipotle powder and/or a 4-ounce can of diced jalapeno or green chiles.

VEGETARIAN GOULASH

3 tablespoons	**olive oil,** divided
28 ounces	**extra-firm tofu,** frozen and thawed, then pressed and cubed
$^1/_4$ cup	**sweet Hungarian paprika,** divided
2	**onions,** finely chopped
2	**red bell peppers,** chopped
5 cloves	**garlic,** minced
2 teaspoons	**caraway seeds**
2 tablespoons	**tomato paste**
3 tablespoons	**red wine vinegar**
$^1/_4$ cup	**flour**
3 cups	**vegetable broth**
$^1/_2$ cup	**sour cream**
	salt and pepper

Preheat oven to 300 degrees.

Heat 2 tablespoons olive oil in a small saute pan over medium heat. Add tofu and toss until coated with oil. Add 2 tablespoons paprika, stirring until well-coated. Saute 5 minutes and set aside. Heat remaining oil in a large Dutch oven. Add onions and bell peppers, cooking until onions soften. Add garlic and saute 2 minutes. Stir in caraway seeds, tomato paste and vinegar and then cook for 1 minute. Add flour and stir about 2 minutes, or until evenly distributed. Add tofu to pan and then slowly stir in the broth. Bring to a simmer, cover and transfer to Dutch oven. Bake for 1 hour in preheated oven. Remove from oven and whisk in the sour cream. Garnish with freshly chopped parsley if desired and season with salt and pepper to taste. Makes 6–8 servings.

VEGAN GUMBO

1/2 cup	**peanut oil**
1/2 cup	**flour**
1 cup each	**diced green bell pepper, onion, and celery**
4 cloves	**garlic,** minced
14 ounces	**firm tofu,** drained and pressed
8 cups	**vegetable broth**
1 pound	**frozen okra**
1 can (15 ounces)	**diced tomatoes,** with liquid
1/2 teaspoon	**thyme**
1/4 teaspoon each	**Tabasco and cayenne pepper**
1/2 tablespoon	**liquid smoke**
1 teaspoon each	**salt and coarse black pepper**
1 teaspoon	**gumbo file or Cajun seasoning**

Combine oil and flour over medium heat in a large cast-iron pan or stockpot. Cook, stirring constantly, until a light golden color, about 20–25 minutes. Add the bell pepper, onion, celery and garlic. Stir until vegetables are coated with flour mixture and beginning to soften. Coarsely chop and add tofu. Add broth and raise heat to high. Add remaining ingredients. Lower heat and simmer for 45 minutes. Serve over rice. Makes 10–12 servings.

CREAMY MUSHROOM SOUP

4 tablespoons	**butter or margarine**
1	**large onion,** chopped
1 pound	**crimini or brown button mushrooms,** sliced
$^1/_2$ teaspoon	**thyme**
$^1/_4$ teaspoon	**nutmeg**
	salt and pepper
2 tablespoons	**flour**
4 cups	**vegetable broth**
16 ounces	**silken tofu**
$^1/_2$ cup	**vegan or regular sour cream**

Melt butter in a large saucepan. Saute onion over medium-high heat until it starts to soften. Add mushrooms and continue sauteeing for 5 minutes. Add seasonings and then whisk in flour, stirring continuously for another 3 minutes. Add broth and reduce heat to low. Let simmer for 10 minutes. Transfer mixture to a blender, add silken tofu and puree until smooth. Return to saucepan, stir in sour cream, and simmer 15 minutes. Makes 4–6 servings.

BUTTERNUT SQUASH SOUP

4 cups	**vegetable broth**
1 cup	**orange juice**
1 large	**butternut squash,** peeled, seeded and cut into chunks
1 large	**shallot,** finely chopped
	salt and pepper
2 tablespoons	**brown sugar**
$1/4$ teaspoon	**nutmeg**
14 ounces	**firm tofu,** pressed and cut into 6 pieces

Combine all ingredients in a large saucepan. Bring liquid to a boil and then reduce heat; cover and let simmer 45 minutes, or until squash is tender. Using a ladle, transfer the chunks of squash, tofu and about 1 cup of the hot liquid to a blender. Puree on high until smooth and then return to the pan, stirring until pureed mixture is completely incorporated. Makes 4–6 servings.

WALDORF SALAD

2 cups	**chopped green apples**
2 cups	**chopped red apples**
I tablespoon	**lemon juice**
2 cups	**chopped celery**
I cup	**chopped walnuts**
8 ounces	**silken tofu**
8 ounces	**vanilla yogurt**
I	**tablespoon sugar,** or more to taste

Toss apple chunks in lemon juice. Add celery and walnuts. In a blender, blend tofu, yogurt and sugar together until smooth. Stir into apple mixture and chill 1–2 hours. Serve cold, mounded on a lettuce leaf, if desired. Makes 6–8 servings.

BROCCOLI MADNESS SALAD

8 cups	**chopped broccoli**
3 cups	**red seedless grapes**
16 ounces	**extra-firm tofu,** drained, pressed and cubed
$^1/_2$ cup	**shelled roasted sunflower seeds**
$^1/_2$ cup	**coarsely chopped roasted cashews**
$^1/_2$ cup	**raisins or dried cranberries**
1 cup	**coleslaw dressing**

Steam broccoli or cook in microwave oven about 3 minutes, or until bright green and just done. Do not overcook. Rinse in cold water and place in a large serving bowl. Cut grapes in half. Add tofu, grapes, sunflower seeds, cashews and raisins to broccoli. Cover and chill at least 2 hours or overnight. Stir in dressing just before serving. Makes 10–12 servings as a side dish.

LAYERED FIESTA CHOPPED SALAD

8 ounces	**extra-firm tofu,** drained and rinsed
I teaspoon	**chipotle chili powder**
I cup	**zesty Italian dressing**
I can (15 ounces)	**black beans,** drained and rinsed
I box (8 ounces)	**frozen corn,** thawed and rinsed
I	**green bell pepper,** diced
I	**red bell pepper,** diced

Cut tofu into very small cubes. Stir chili powder into dressing. Toss each ingredient with dressing and then, using a slotted spoon, layer one at a time in a medium glass bowl or trifle dish. Cover and refrigerate 1–2 hours, or until well chilled. Makes 8–10 servings as a side dish.

MOCK CHICKEN SALAD

14 ounces	**firm tofu,** drained and pressed
¹/₄ cup	**soy sauce**
1 cup	**water**
1	**red bell pepper,** diced
3 stalks	**celery,** diced
¹/₂	**red onion,** finely chopped
1 cup	**Tofu Mayonnaise** (see Sauces, Dressings, and Spreads, page 24)
1 teaspoon	**paprika**
¹/₂ teaspoon each	**basil and oregano**
	salt and pepper

Preheat oven to 350 degrees.

Cut tofu into ¹/₂-inch squares, then cut diagonally across the squares to form triangles. In a small baking dish, combine tofu and soy sauce with water; marinate 15 minutes. Bake 30 minutes and then discard the soy sauce and water marinade; set tofu aside to cool in refrigerator. Combine all remaining ingredients and stir in tofu. Chill until ready to serve. Serve anywhere you would use regular chicken salad, such as on croissants, crackers or sandwich bread. Makes 4–6 servings.

EGGLESS SALAD

14 ounces	**extra-firm tofu,** drained and pressed
1/4 cup	**Tofu Mayonnaise** (see Sauces, Dressings and Spreads, page 24)
1 stalk	**celery,** finely chopped
1 tablespoon	**mustard**
1 teaspoon	**lemon juice**
few dashes	**turmeric**
1/2 teaspoon	**salt**
2 teaspoons	**pickle relish**

Squeeze tofu through hands into a mixing bowl until the texture resembles scrambled eggs with no large chunks left. Thoroughly stir in remaining ingredients. Fill sandwiches, stuff scooped-out tomatoes or serve on large gourmet crackers. Makes 4–6 servings.

CREAMY PASTA SALAD

1 bag (16 ounces)	**rotini or shell pasta,** cooked and cooled
1 box (8 ounces)	**frozen peas,** thawed
1 cup	**grated cheddar cheese**
1/2	**red onion,** minced
1/2	**red bell pepper,** diced
1 can (2.25 ounces)	**sliced black olives,** drained
8 ounces	**silken tofu**
1 cup	**Italian dressing**

Toss cooked pasta, peas, cheese, onion, bell pepper and olives in a medium bowl. Blend tofu and dressing in a blender. Stir blended dressing into pasta mixture. Cover and refrigerate 1–2 hours, or until well chilled. Makes 6–8 servings.

BREAKFAST

SIMPLE TOFU SCRAMBLE

I	**yellow onion,** diced
2 tablespoons	**olive oil**
I	**carrot,** diced
I stalk	**celery,** diced
I4 ounces	**firm or extra-firm tofu,** drained and crumbled
I teaspoon each	**turmeric and cumin**
I tablespoon	**malt or balsamic vinegar**
$^1/_2$ tablespoon	**soy sauce**
	salt and fresh pepper

In a large skillet, saute onion in oil for 2 minutes, or until softened. Add carrot and celery and then saute 3 minutes more. Mix in tofu, spices, vinegar and soy sauce; continue stirring for 3–4 minutes. Season with salt and pepper to taste. Serve with ketchup if desired. Makes 4 servings.

BREAKFAST BURRITOS

I	**red bell pepper,** chopped
$^1/_4$ cup	**chopped green onion**
2 tablespoons	**olive oil**
I can (20 ounces)	**black beans,** drained and rinsed
$^1/_2$ teaspoon	**chili powder**
	Simple Tofu Scramble (see Breakfast, page 50)
8	**medium flour tortillas**
2 cups	**guacamole,** divided
2 cups	**grated cheddar or Monterey Jack cheese**

In a medium-size skillet, saute the bell pepper and green onion in oil over medium heat for 2–3 minutes, or until softened. Add black beans and chili powder and simmer another 2–3 minutes. Stir in the Simple Tofu Scramble mixture and remove from heat. Lay out a tortilla. Spread about $^1/_4$ cup guacamole down the center and then spoon about $^1/_2$ cup of the tofu mixture over the guacamole. Sprinkle about $^1/_4$ cup cheese over top and roll up, folding ends in. Serve with salsa and/or sour cream if desired. Makes 8 servings.

CONFETTI HASH BROWN CASSEROLE

16 ounces	**sharp cheddar cheese**
¹/₂ cup each	**diced green and red bell peppers**
¹/₂ cup	**diced green onions**
5 cups	**frozen hash browns**
4	**eggs**
16 ounces	**silken tofu**
1 teaspoon	**seasoned salt**

Preheat oven to 350 degrees.

Cut cheese into ¹/₄-inch cubes. Mix bell peppers, onion, hash browns and cheese in a large mixing bowl. Spray a 9 x 13-inch baking pan with nonstick cooking spray. Spread mixture in pan. Blend eggs, tofu and salt in a food processor or blender. Pour over hash brown mixture. Bake for 50–60 minutes, or until lightly golden brown on top. Makes 6–8 servings.

UPSIDE-DOWN SKILLET CAKE

2 cups	**diced fresh fruit***
1/4 cup	**sugar**
1 tablespoon	**cinnamon**
1/4 cup	**canola oil**
2 cups	**dry pancake mix**
1 cup	**water**
8 ounces	**silken tofu**
	syrup, as desired

Toss fruit with sugar and cinnamon. Using a 10- to 12-inch skillet or frying pan with a lid, pour in oil. Spread fruit evenly in pan, covering the bottom completely. Blend the pancake mix, water and tofu in a food processor or blender. Pour batter over fruit and spread evenly so the entire surface is covered. Place lid firmly on pan. Cook on stovetop over medium heat for 5 minutes, then without removing lid, reduce heat to low and cook another 10 minutes. Lift lid to assess doneness in center of cake. If necessary, replace lid and turn off heat and let sit another few minutes. When cake is firm in the center, immediately invert onto large serving platter. Cut into wedges to serve and drizzle with syrup. Makes 6–8 servings.

*Use fresh fruits that cook well, such as apples, pears and peaches. Frozen unthawed berries work well also, used exclusively or mixed with fresh fruit. Canned pineapple (chunks or slices) with a few maraschino cherries is also an excellent choice.

TEX-MEX MIGAS

I tablespoon	**canola oil**
1/2	**yellow onion,** finely chopped
I	**jalapeno,** minced
2	**scallions,** chopped
1/4 teaspoon	**soy sauce**
1/4 teaspoon	**turmeric**
14 ounces	**firm tofu,** frozen, thawed and crumbled
I cup	**grated Monterey Jack, sharp cheddar cheese, or soy cheese**
I can (14 ounces)	**diced tomatoes,** drained
2 cups	**crumbled tortilla chips**

Heat the oil in a large frying pan. Saute onion over medium-high heat for 2 minutes. Stir in jalapeno, scallions, soy sauce and turmeric. Add tofu and stir-fry until tofu is coated in seasonings. Add cheese, tomatoes and chips. Stir until all ingredients are well-combined and cheese has melted. Makes 4–6 servings.

VARIATION: After tofu is added to pan, stir in 2 tablespoons chopped fresh cilantro and Tabasco sauce to taste.

ANY FRUIT QUICK BREAD

I cup	**sugar**
$^1/_4$ cup	**butter**
I$^2/_3$ cups	**mashed fruit***
$^1/_2$ cup	**silken tofu**
I	**egg**
2 cups	**flour**
I teaspoon	**baking soda**
I teaspoon	**salt**
$^1/_2$ cup	**chopped walnuts** (optional)

Preheat oven to 350 degrees.

Cream sugar and butter in a mixing bowl. Add mashed fruit, tofu and egg. Add dry ingredients and nuts, if desired. Pour into a greased loaf pan. Bake 60–70 minutes, or until firm and lightly browned. Makes 8–10 slices.

*Applesauce or canned pumpkin works well here, or use mashed bananas, strawberries or raspberries.

SMOOTHIES

For each recipe, combine all ingredients in a blender, using high speed. Each recipe makes 3–4 servings.

Honey Berry Blast:

$1/2$ cup	**frozen blueberries**
$1/2$ cup	**frozen strawberries**
1	**banana**
$1/2$ cup	**silken tofu**
$1/2$ cup	**soy milk or orange juice**
2 to 3 tablespoons	**honey**
4	**ice cubes**

Healthy Elvis:

$1/2$ cup	**peanut butter**
1	**frozen banana**
$1/2$ cup	**silken tofu**
$1/2$ cup	**soy milk**
2 tablespoons	**ground golden flaxmeal**
1 tablespoon	**honey** (optional)
5 to 6	**ice cubes**

Date Shake:

$1/2$ cup	**pitted dates**
$1/2$ cup	**silken tofu**
$1/4$ cup	**soy milk**
6	**ice cubes**
	dash of nutmeg

Chocolate Peanut Butter Cream:

$1/2$ cup	**peanut butter**
1	**frozen banana**
$1/2$ cup	**silken tofu**
$1/2$ cup	**soy milk**
3 tablespoons	**chocolate syrup**
5 to 6	**ice cubes**

APPLE STREUSEL COFFEE CAKE

1/2 cup	**light brown sugar**
1/2 cup	**finely chopped walnuts**
2 1/4 cups	**flour,** divided
1 teaspoon	**cinnamon**
1/2 cup	**butter or margarine,** melted and divided
1/2 cup	**quick-cooking oatmeal**
1 teaspoon each	**baking powder, baking soda and salt**
16 ounces	**silken tofu**
1/2 cup	**sugar**
2	**eggs or equivalent egg substitute**
1 teaspoon	**vanilla**
2 cups	**peeled and chopped baking apples**

Preheat oven to 350 degrees.

In a small bowl, combine brown sugar, nuts, 1/4 cup flour, cinnamon and 2 tablespoons melted butter. Blend oatmeal in a blender until fine crumbs. Add to sugar mixture and set aside.

In a medium bowl, combine remaining flour, powder, soda and salt. In blender, blend tofu, remaining butter, sugar, eggs and vanilla. Add to dry mixture. Spread dough in a greased 9 x 13-inch baking pan. Sprinkle apples over top and then press into dough. Sprinkle brown sugar mixture over top. Bake 40–50 minutes, or until lightly browned; serve warm. Makes 10–12 servings.

VARIATION: Replace apples with chopped peaches, blueberries or pears.

TOFU BENEDICT

8 cups	**coarsely chopped spinach**
2 teaspoons	**minced garlic**
1 teaspoon	**salt,** divided
$^1/_2$ cup	**canola oil,** divided
16 ounces	**button mushrooms,** sliced
3	**English muffins,** halved and toasted
	Healthy Hollandaise Sauce, (see Sauces, Dressings and Spreads, page 31)
	Tofu Filets, (see Main Dishes, page 74)

Saute spinach, garlic and $^1/_2$ teaspoon salt in $^1/_4$ cup oil; set aside. Saute mushrooms in remaining oil and salt; set aside. Layer on individual serving plates the following: $^1/_2$ English muffin, $^1/_2$ cup spinach, 1 Tofu Filet and $^1/_2$ cup mushrooms. Pour $^1/_2$ cup Healthy Hollandaise Sauce over top. Microwave for 60–90 seconds, or until hot; serve immediately. Makes 6 servings.

MIX 'N' MATCH MUFFINS

¹/₂ cup	**melted butter**
I cup	**sugar**
16 ounces	**silken tofu**
3	**eggs**
I tablespoon	**baking powder**
I teaspoon each	**baking soda and salt**
3¹/₂ cups	**flour**
I teaspoon	**almond extract, vanilla extract, poppy seeds, lemon zest, orange zest or cinnamon**
1¹/₂ cups	**fruit and/or nuts***

Preheat oven to 375 degrees.

Using a hand mixer, cream the butter and sugar together. Add tofu and eggs and mix until smooth. Add remaining ingredients in order listed, mixing by hand until just barely mixed. Batter will be slightly lumpy. Bake in greased muffin tins 30–40 minutes, or until firm and browned. Makes 12 muffins.

*Use any of the following in any combination
Nuts: sliced almonds, chopped pecans or walnuts
Frozen fruits: raspberries, blueberries or blackberries
Fresh diced fruits: apples, pears or peaches
Dried fruits: raisins, cranberries, cherries or diced apricots

VEGAN FRENCH TOAST

¹/₂ cup	**firm tofu**
I cup	**vanilla soy milk**
I ¹/₂ teaspoons	**vanilla**
I teaspoon	**cinnamon**
	dash of turmeric
I0	**slices bread**

Blend all ingredients except bread in a blender. Pour into in a pie pan
or small baking dish. Dip each slice of bread in the mixture and then
place on a heated frying pan that has been sprayed with nonstick
cooking spray or lightly buttered. Cook 4 minutes on each side, or
until each side is browned and firm. Serve with syrup and any other
desired toppings. Makes 4–6 servings.

KIDS' FAVORITES

HEALTHY MAC 'N' CHEESE

1 bag (16 ounces)	**regular or whole wheat elbow macaroni**
16 ounces	**silken tofu**
1/2 cup	**evaporated milk**
2 teaspoons	**seasoned salt**
1 tablespoon	**butter-flavored granules**
16 ounces	**sharp cheddar cheese,** grated

Cook macaroni according to package directions; drain and set aside. In a blender, add tofu one spoonful at a time to milk, blending until smooth; add seasoned salt and butter granules. Pour tofu mixture into pan and cook over medium heat until bubbly. Slowly add cheese, stirring until melted. Stir in macaroni and cook for 3–5 minutes, stirring constantly. Remove from heat and let sit for a few minutes before serving. Makes 6–8 servings.

TOFU TOES

14 ounces	**firm tofu,** frozen, thawed and drained
$^1/_2$ cup	**cornmeal**
$^1/_2$ teaspoon	**salt**
1 teaspoon	**garlic powder**
$^1/_4$ teaspoon	**paprika**
few dashes	**parsley flakes**
	salt and pepper

Preheat oven to 425 degrees.

Liberally coat a baking sheet with nonstick spray. Thoroughly press all excess water from tofu. Slice the tofu lengthwise into 6 strips, and then across into 4, about the size of a child's big toe. Mix the cornmeal and seasonings together. Roll the toes in the mixture until well-covered and set $^1/_2$ inch apart on baking sheet. (If the cornmeal isn't sticking, lightly spray the toes themselves with a little of the spray and then give the toes an extra roll in the coating.)

Bake 20 minutes, or until golden brown, using tongs to turn over after 10 minutes. Season with more salt and pepper if desired and then serve with your favorite barbecue sauce, honey mustard, ketchup, tartar sauce or ranch dressing. Makes about 2 dozen.

TOFU SLOPPY JOES

1/2 cup	**diced onion**
1/2 cup	**diced green bell pepper**
1/4 cup	**butter or margarine**
14 ounces	**extra-firm tofu,** frozen and thawed
1 can (6 ounces)	**tomato paste**
1/4 cup	**brown sugar**
2 tablespoons	**vinegar**
1/4 cup	**soy sauce**
1 teaspoon	**garlic powder**
1 cup	**water**
8	**hamburger buns**

In a large frying pan, saute onion and bell pepper in butter over medium heat for 2–3 minutes. Press tofu dry and crumble into pan, cooking another 5 minutes and stirring constantly. Add remaining ingredients except buns and simmer 8–10 minutes more, stirring constantly to remove moisture. Serve on buns with a slice of cheddar cheese on top if desired. Makes 8 servings.

NUTTERBALLS

I cup	**uncooked brown rice**
2 cups	**water**
14 ounces	**firm tofu,** drained and squeezed
4 tablespoons	**soy sauce**
I cup	**ground almonds**
I cup	**plain breadcrumbs**
4 tablespoons	**chunky peanut butter**
I teaspoon	**salt**

Preheat oven to 350 degrees.

In a small saucepan, bring the rice to a boil in water. Cover and reduce heat to a low simmer. Cook until water is absorbed and rice is soft and sticky, about 40 minutes. In a blender or food processor, combine tofu, soy sauce and about 2 cups cooked rice. Blend until thick and pasty. Spoon blended mixture and remaining rice into mixing bowl and then add almonds, breadcrumbs, peanut butter and salt; mix well.

Spray a baking sheet with nonstick spray. Hand-roll the mixture (or use a melon baller to scoop) into little balls, about I ¹/₂ inches thick. Bake for 30–40 minutes, or until browned. Serve as an appetizer or a snack. Makes 8–10 servings.

FLUFFY PEANUT BUTTER SPREAD

7 ounces **extra-firm tofu,** drained
2 cups **creamy peanut butter**
$1/4$ cup **honey**

Blend all ingredients in a food processor or blender until well blended. Use in place of peanut butter on sandwiches, crackers, celery sticks, apple slices, etc. Store in an airtight container in the refrigerator for up to 2 weeks. Makes 3 cups.

PEANUT BUTTER MINI PIZZA VARIATION: Toast half an English muffin and cool. Spread with a thin layer of the peanut butter spread. Place a few banana slices on top to resemble pepperoni pizza. Sprinkle with coconut to resemble grated mozzarella cheese.

HEALTHY ANTS ON A LOG VARIATION: Fill the cavity of a stalk of celery with the peanut butter spread. Place raisins or cranberries on top.

HI-PRO-TATOES (HIGH-PROTEIN MASHED POTATOES)

2	**large potatoes,** peeled and quartered
$1/4$ cup	**olive oil**
5 cloves	**garlic,** peeled
14 ounces	**extra-firm tofu,** drained and pressed
$1 1/2$ teaspoons	**salt,** or more to taste
	coarsely ground black pepper
3 tablespoons	**chopped fresh chives** (optional)

Boil potatoes until they give no resistance when poked with a knife, about 40 minutes. While boiling, heat oil and garlic in a small saute pan over low heat. Stir frequently until garlic is soft and lightly golden, about 5 minutes. Place tofu in a food processor, add garlic and oil and then puree together until smooth; set aside.

When potatoes are done, drain water and return potatoes to their pot. Mash with a ricer or fork to desired consistency, then add tofu-garlic mixture. Season with salt and pepper, and garnish with fresh chives if desired. Makes 4 servings.

SNACK PARFAITS

I cup	**vanilla yogurt**
7 ounces	**firm tofu,** drained
I tablespoon	**sugar or honey**
4 cups	**granola or other favorite cereal,** divided
4 cups	**chopped fresh berries and fruit,** divided
4 tablespoons	**chopped nuts,** divided

In a blender mix yogurt, tofu and sugar or honey. In 4 large wide-mouth glasses or small glass bowls, layer $1/2$ cup granola, $1/2$ cup fruit and $1/3$ cup tofu mixture. Repeat process. Sprinkle I tablespoon nuts on top as a garnish. Makes 4 servings.

MAIN DISHES

TOFU FILETS

$^1/_4$ cup **balsamic vinegar**
3 tablespoons **soy sauce**
1 teaspoon **garlic powder**
1 teaspoon **liquid smoke**
16 ounces **extra-firm tofu,** drained and pressed

Preheat oven to 350 degrees.

Mix first four ingredients together. Pour half the mixture into a 9 x
9-inch baking pan. Slice tofu into 6 slices width wise, about $^1/_2$ inch
thick. Lay slices in pan, completely filling pan. Pour remaining sauce
over tofu. Bake 30 minutes, basting once or twice while baking.
Remove from oven and turn tofu slices over. Bake another 30 minutes,
basting once or twice while baking; serve warm. Refrigerate leftover
filets in a zipper-lock bag for up to 1 week. Makes 4–6 servings.

GROUND TOFU FILLING

¹/₄ cup	**soy sauce**
1 tablespoon	**creamy peanut butter**
1 teaspoon	**cumin**
1 teaspoon	**garlic powder**
1 teaspoon	**liquid smoke**
1 teaspoon	**chili powder**
16 ounces	**extra-firm tofu,** frozen, thawed and pressed dry
3 tablespoons	**canola oil**

Preheat oven to 350 degrees.

Mix first six ingredients together in a medium-size bowl. Crumble tofu into bowl and stir to coat. Spread oil onto a large baking sheet and sprinkle tofu mixture evenly over oil. Bake for 20 minutes. Remove from oven and stir. Bake 20–30 minutes more, or until liquid has evaporated and tofu resembles cooked hamburger meat. This filling can be used in tacos, burritos, casseroles or anywhere you would normally use ground beef. Makes 1¹/₂ cups filling.

HOMEMADE VEGGIE BURGERS

Ground Tofu Filling (see Main Dishes, page 71)
$^1/_2$ **yellow onion,** grated
1 **green bell pepper,** minced
$^1/_2$ cup **cooked brown rice**
$^1/_2$ cup **seasoned breadcrumbs**
1 **egg,** beaten

Using hands, thoroughly combine all ingredients. Form into 4–6 patties. Coat a frying pan with nonstick spray and then cook each patty over medium heat about 3 minutes per side. Serve as a substitute for beef burgers. Makes 4–6 servings.

VARIATION: For a spicier version, use chipotle powder in place of regular chili powder for the Ground Tofu Filling recipe, then add 1 teaspoon crushed red pepper flakes and $^1/_2$ teaspoon Tabasco sauce to the patty mixture.

THREE-CHEESE STUFFED SHELLS

I box (12 ounces)	**jumbo pasta shells**
8 ounces	**firm tofu,** drained and crumbled
$^{1}/_{2}$ cup	**ricotta cheese**
$^{1}/_{2}$ cup	**grated Parmesan cheese**
I cup	**coarsely grated mozzarella cheese**
I	**egg,** beaten with fork
2 tablespoons	**dried minced parsley**
2 teaspoons	**garlic powder**
I teaspoon	**salt**
I jar (26 ounces)	**spaghetti sauce**

Preheat oven to 400 degrees.

Cook pasta shells according to package directions; rinse in cold water and set aside. Combine all remaining ingredients, except spaghetti sauce, in a mixing bowl. Pour I cup spaghetti sauce in a 9 x 13-inch baking pan. Fill each pasta shell with about 2 tablespoons cheese mixture. Place stuffed shells in pan. Pour remaining spaghetti sauce over top and then bake 40–50 minutes, or until bubbly. Serve hot with additional Parmesan cheese as a garnish.

TRICOLOR QUICHE

1 cup	**diced yellow bell pepper**
2 cloves	**garlic,** minced
2 tablespoons	**olive oil**
2 cups	**chopped broccoli florets**
1/4 cup	**minced roasted red peppers**
14 ounces	**firm tofu,** drained and pressed
1/2 cup	**soy milk**
1/2 teaspoon	**basil**
6 ounces	**sharp cheddar or soy cheese,** grated
1 (9-inch)	**unbaked piecrust**

Preheat oven to 425 degrees.

In a large frying pan, saute yellow peppers and garlic in oil over medi-um-high heat for 2 minutes. Add broccoli and roasted red peppers and cook a few minutes more, stirring occasionally, until broccoli is bright green but not soft; set aside.

Crumble tofu into a blender. Add soy milk and basil; blend together until smooth (it might be a little grainy). Pour into mixing bowl. Stir grated cheese into soy mixture and then stir in the vegetables. Pour entire mixture into piecrust. Sprinkle fresh black pepper over top, if desired. Bake 50 minutes, or until the top is golden brown. Makes 6–8 servings.

CHEESE FONDUE

16 ounces	**silken tofu**
2 teaspoons	**garlic salt**
$^1/_2$ cup	**dry white wine or white grape juice**
16 ounces	**Swiss cheese,** grated
10 to 12 cups	**vegetable chunks,** lightly steamed*
1 loaf	**French bread,** cubed

In a medium saucepan, cook tofu, garlic salt and juice over medium heat until bubbling. Add cheese a handful at a time and continue cooking until melted. Pour mixture into a blender and blend on high about 1 minute, or until smooth. Pour into a fondue pot and serve warm with vegetables and bread cubes for dipping. Makes 6–8 servings.

*Try broccoli, cauliflower, squash, bell peppers, mushrooms or red potatoes.

VARIATION: Substitute sharp cheddar cheese for Swiss cheese.

FESTIVE CRESCENT WREATH

2 tubes (10 ounces each)	**ready-to-bake crescent rolls**
2 cups	**grated pepper jack cheese**
14 ounces	**extra-firm tofu,** frozen and thawed
1 cup	**diced fresh broccoli**
1/2 cup	**diced red bell pepper**
1/4 cup	**diced green onion**
1 teaspoon	**garlic powder**
1 teaspoon	**seasoned salt**

Preheat oven to 375 degrees.

Press tofu dry and crumble into mixing bowl. Unroll crescent rolls and arrange on a 15-inch round pizza pan, with wide edges of dough triangles about 2 inches in from outside edge of pan and the pointed edges hanging off pan. Wide edges of dough triangles should overlap about 2 inches. Mix remaining ingredients with tofu and spoon onto top of wide edges of dough circle, all the way around the circle. Bring pointed edges of dough up and fold over the tofu mixture and tuck into inside circle of dough. Some filling will be showing between each section of dough. Bake 20–25 minutes, or until golden brown. Makes 6–8 servings.

VEGGIE CALZONE

1/2 cup	**diced green onions**
1/4 cup	**canola oil**
2 cups	**diced shiitake or brown mushrooms**
1 box (10 ounces)	**frozen chopped spinach,** thawed and drained
14 ounces	**extra-firm tofu,** frozen, thawed and drained
2 teaspoons	**garlic salt**
1/2 cup	**grated Parmesan cheese**
2 tubes (10 ounces each)	**refrigerated pizza dough**
1 jar (26 ounces)	**spaghetti sauce**

Preheat oven to 375 degrees.

Saute onions in oil until translucent, about 2 minutes. Add mushrooms and spinach and cook another 3–5 minutes, or until liquid has evaporated. Crumble the tofu and add. Remove from heat and add garlic salt and cheese. Unroll pizza dough rectangles on a floured surface. Cut into 8-inch squares. Place 1/2 cup tofu mixture in center and fold dough over top to form a triangle. Pinch edges of dough together to secure. Place each triangle on a greased baking sheet. Bake 25–30 minutes, or until lightly browned. Heat spaghetti sauce and pour over each triangle when serving. Makes 8 servings.

MUSHROOM STRUDEL

16 ounces	**brown button mushrooms,** minced
1 teaspoon each	**salt and garlic powder**
4	**green onions,** minced
1/4 cup	**butter or margarine**
14 ounces	**extra-firm tofu,** drained and pressed
1/4 cup	**grated Parmesan cheese**
1 box (17 ounces)	**frozen puff pastry,** thawed

Preheat oven to 375 degrees.

Saute mushrooms, spices and onions in butter for 2–3 minutes. Crumble tofu and stir in; cook another 3–5 minutes, or until liquid has evaporated. Remove from heat and cool to room temperature; stir in cheese. Place 1 of the 2 pastry sheets on a nonstick or lightly-floured surface. Spread 1 cup mushroom mixture on three-fourths of the pastry's surface, beginning 1 inch from closest edge. Roll jelly roll–style and then slice into 2-inch-thick slices and place cut edge down on a baking sheet sprayed with nonstick spray. Repeat this process with the other sheet of pastry. Bake 30–40 minutes, or until mushroom spirals are browned; serve warm. Makes 6–8 servings.

ROASTED VEGETABLE LAYERED CASSEROLE

2 each	**red and green bell peppers**
6	**medium zucchini**
1/4 cup	**olive oil**
14 ounces	**firm tofu,** drained, pressed and crumbled
1/2 cup each	**ricotta and grated Parmesan cheese**
1 teaspoon	**garlic salt**
1 tablespoon	**dried parsley flakes**
1 cup	**spaghetti sauce or tomato sauce**

Preheat oven to 350 degrees.

Cut vegetables lengthwise into long 1/4-inch-thick planks. Lay vegetables in a single layer on a baking sheet and brush with olive oil. Broil under high heat for 3–5 minutes, or until browned. Turn vegetables over and broil another 3 minutes, or until browned.

In a small bowl, mix tofu, cheeses, garlic salt and parsley flakes; set aside. Spread 1/2 cup spaghetti sauce in bottom of a 9 x 13-inch baking pan. Layer the following in order: one-third of the vegetables, half the tofu mixture, one-third of the vegetables, remaining tofu mixture, remaining vegetables and then the remaining spaghetti sauce. Bake 40–50 minutes, or until cooked through and bubbly. Makes 6–8 servings.

ITALIAN-STYLE "MEAT LOAF"

1 tablespoon	**extra virgin olive oil**
1	**small onion,** grated
3 cloves	**garlic,** minced
2 cups	**frozen soy protein crumbles**
$^1/_4$ cup	**red wine or red wine vinegar**
1 tablespoon	**Worcestershire sauce** (vegetarian, if available)
14 ounces	**firm tofu,** drained and pressed
10 ounces	**frozen spinach,** thawed
1	**egg white or egg replacement**
$^1/_2$ cup	**breadcrumbs**
1 can (6 ounces)	**tomato paste,** divided
1 teaspoon each	**dried basil, oregano and salt**
1 teaspoon	**ground black pepper**

Preheat oven to 375 degrees.

Heat a frying pan with oil. Add onion and saute until softened, about 3–4 minutes. Mix in garlic and saute another minute. Add soy crumbles and stir until combined. Pour in red wine and cook 3 minutes. Stir in Worcestershire and set aside.

In a large mixing bowl, thoroughly squeeze the tofu through your hands until there are no large chunks left. Add the spinach, egg white, breadcrumbs, 3 tablespoons tomato paste and seasonings. Combine well. Add soy crumble mixture into the bowl and combine again. Press firmly into an $8^1/_2$ x $4^1/_2$-inch loaf pan coated with nonstick spray and smooth the top. Cover with foil and bake for 35 minutes. Remove foil and spread remaining tomato paste over top. Sprinkle with additional salt and pepper to taste. Bake another 15 minutes and let cool in pan for 15 minutes before serving. Makes 6–8 servings.

VEGGIE STIR-FRY

¹/₄ cup	**canola oil,** divided
2 tablespoons	**peanut or sesame oil,** divided
14 ounces	**extra-firm tofu,** drained and pressed dry
1 cup	**teriyaki stir-fry sauce,** divided
2 cups	**chopped celery**
2 cups	**chopped bell peppers and/or onions**
1 cup	**pea pods,** halved
1 cup	**sliced mushrooms**
1 can (4 ounces)	**sliced water chestnuts,** drained and chopped in half
1 tablespoon	**cornstarch**

Pour half the canola oil and half the peanut oil into a large wok. Heat to medium heat. Cut tofu into small cubes the size of dice. Stir-fry cubes in two batches until well browned, about 3 minutes. Place cooked cubes in a small bowl and toss with 2 tablespoons of the stir-fry sauce. Add remaining oils to wok and heat to medium-high heat. Add celery and stir-fry for 1 minute. Add peppers and stir-fry another minute. Add pea pods, mushrooms and water chestnuts and stir-fry 2 minutes more. Stir cornstarch into remaining stir-fry sauce and then stir into wok mixture. Add tofu cubes and stir gently. Serve over cooked rice. Makes 4–6 servings.

KUNG PAO VARIATION: Use 4 cups celery, 2 cups onions and 1 cup unsalted shelled peanuts. Stir 2 tablespoons peanut butter into stir-fry sauce.

SWEET AND SOUR VARIATION: In place of mushrooms, use 1 can (16 ounces) drained pineapple tidbits. Use a sweet and sour stir-fry sauce in place of teriyaki sauce.

TOFU MINI POTPIES

I tube (16 ounces)	**Pillsbury Grands Flaky Layers Biscuits**
2 tablespoons	**butter or margarine**
I stalk	**celery,** diced
I	**medium onion,** diced
I	**large carrot,** diced
2 cups	**vegetable broth**
14 ounces	**extra-firm tofu,** frozen, thawed and pressed then diced into $1/2$-inch cubes
I teaspoon each	**dried thyme and parsley**
$3/4$ cup	**light cream**
I	**large potato,** peeled and diced
I cup	**frozen peas**
	salt and pepper, to taste

Preheat oven to 375 degrees.

Spray 8 muffin cups with nonstick spray. Separate dough into 8 biscuits; divide each biscuit into 2 layers. Place 8 halves in muffin cups, stretching and pressing to cover bottom and up the sides. Set remaining halves aside.

Melt butter in a large saucepan over medium-high heat. Add the celery, onion, and carrot; saute 5 minutes. Add broth and bring to a boil. Add tofu, thyme and parsley, stirring well to combine. Reduce heat to medium-low and simmer 15 minutes, or until reduced by half. Add cream and return to a boil. Add potatoes and cook until tender, about 10 minutes. Stir in peas and season with salt and pepper. Remove from heat. Spoon mixture into the biscuit halves in the muffin tin. Place remaining biscuit halves over top and pinch edges to seal. Bake 15–18 minutes, or until edges are golden brown. Let cool slightly in muffin tin before removing. Makes 8 servings.

VEGETARIAN SHEPHERD'S PIE

2 tablespoons	**olive oil**
1	**large onion,** chopped
14 ounces	**extra-firm tofu,** frozen, thawed and crumbled
4 cloves	**garlic,** minced
1 cup each	**finely chopped mushrooms, parsnip, eggplant and green bell pepper**
2 tablespoons	**vegetarian Worcestershire sauce**
2 teaspoons	**dried basil**
1/2 teaspoon each	**dried thyme, oregano and paprika**
1/3 cup	**seasoned breadcrumbs**
1 cup	**frozen peas**
3 tablespoons	**balsamic vinegar**
6 cups	**mashed potatoes**

Preheat oven to 350 degrees.

In a large frying pan, heat oil over medium heat; add onion and cook until it begins to soften, about 4 minutes. Add crumbled tofu, garlic and vegetables, except peas and mashed potatoes. Add Worcestershire and seasonings; cook 10 minutes, stirring occasionally. Stir in breadcrumbs, peas and vinegar. Spread vegetable/tofu mixture into bottom of a lightly greased 9 x 13-inch glass baking dish. Spread mashed potatoes over top. Bake 30 minutes. Makes 6 servings.

VARIATION: Garnish with 1/2 cup grated sharp cheddar or soy cheese and a few dashes paprika; top with coarse black pepper.

TOFU TAMALE PIE

Filling:

	Ground Tofu Filling, (see Main Dishes, page 75)
I can (29 ounces)	**pinto beans,** with liquid
I can (14 ounces)	**diced tomatoes and green chiles,** with liquid
I can (6 ounces)	**tomato paste**
I	**whole yellow onion,** diced
2 cups	**frozen corn**
$^1/_4$ cup	**soy sauce**
I teaspoon	**chili powder**
2 cups	**grated cheddar cheese**

Topping:

I cup	**cornmeal**
I cup	**regular or whole wheat flour**
2 teaspoons	**baking powder**
I cup	**milk**
I	**egg**

Preheat oven to 350 degrees.

Simmer all filling ingredients except cheese on stovetop for 10–12 minutes, or until slightly thickened. Remove from heat and stir in cheese. Pour into a 2$^1/_2$-quart baking dish. Mix together topping ingredients and pour over top. Bake 50–60 minutes, or until lightly browned on top. Makes 8–10 servings.

TOFU STROGANOFF

2 tablespoons	**tomato paste**
2 cups	**vegetable broth,** divided
2 tablespoons	**olive oil**
I	**large onion,** diced
I4 ounces	**extra-firm tofu,** pressed and cut into 2-inch strips
I0 ounces	**mushrooms,** sliced
2 tablespoons	**flour**
2 tablespoons	**paprika**
	coarsely ground black pepper
I teaspoon	**Dijon mustard**
I cup	**sour cream** (regular or non-dairy)

Combine tomato paste and $^1/_2$ cup broth in a small bowl and set aside. Heat oil over medium heat in a large saucepan. Saute onion until it begins to soften. Add the tofu and mushrooms and cook 3 minutes more. Stir in the flour and paprika and cook about I minute, or until well integrated. Add the tomato paste mixture and stir until smooth and incorporated. Add remaining broth, pepper, and mustard; bring to a boil. Reduce to a simmer and cook, covered, for 20 minutes, or until sauce has thickened. Stir in sour cream until smooth. Serve over egg noodles or basmati rice. Makes 4–6 servings.

SUBLIME SPINACH LASAGNA

I box (10 ounces)	**frozen chopped spinach,** thawed, pressed and drained
14 ounces	**soft tofu,** drained, pressed and squeezed
3 cloves	**garlic,** minced
I teaspoon	**dried minced onion**
$^1/_4$ cup	**silken tofu**
$^1/_2$ cup	**grated Parmesan cheese or soy Parmesan substitute,** divided
	salt and freshly ground pepper
2 jars (26 ounces each)	**marinara sauce**
I package (9 ounces)	**no-boil lasagna noodles**
16 ounces	**mozzarella cheese or soy mozzarella,** grated

Preheat oven to 375 degrees.

In a large mixing bowl, combine spinach with soft tofu, garlic, and onion. Add silken tofu, $^1/_4$ cup Parmesan cheese, salt and pepper. In a 9 x 13-inch pan lightly coated with nonstick spray, pour a bit of marinara sauce to cover bottom of pan.

Lay 4 of the lasagna noodles in bottom of pan, overlapping slightly. Spread half the tofu mixture over top, covering completely. Sprinkle $^3/_4$ cup mozzarella cheese over the tofu and then pour about I cup marinara sauce over top; repeat layers. On the final layer, use only 3 noodles, then the remaining sauce and then top with a sprinkling of mozzarella cheese and some of the remaining Parmesan cheese. Cover with foil and bake 45 minutes. Remove foil and then cook another 15 minutes, or until bubbly. Serve topped with extra Parmesan cheese and fresh parsley if desired. Makes 8 servings.

TOFU PARMIGIANA

2 blocks (14 ounces each)	**extra-firm tofu,** drained and pressed
$1/2$ cup	**flour**
	salt and pepper, to taste
2	**eggs**
1 tablespoon	**milk**
1 cup	**seasoned breadcrumbs**
$1 1/4$ cups	**grated Parmesan cheese,** divided
1 tablespoon	**garlic powder**
$1/2$ cup	**chopped fresh parsley**
3 tablespoons	**olive oil**
1 jar (28 ounces)	**marinara sauce**
8 ounces	**fresh mozzarella,** thinly sliced

Slice the blocks of tofu in half lengthwise, creating 4 rectangular cutlets. Put the flour in a shallow platter and season with salt and pepper; combine thoroughly. In a large bowl, beat eggs and milk with a fork until frothy. Place breadcrumbs on a plate and add 1 cup Parmesan, garlic powder and parsley. Season with salt and pepper and stir to combine.

Preheat oven to 350 F. Heat the oil over medium-high heat in a large ovenproof skillet. Lightly dredge both sides of the tofu in the seasoned flour and then dip in eggs mixture to coat, allowing excess to drip off. Dredge in the breadcrumb mixture and then place in the skillet and fry 4 minutes on each side, or until golden and crusty.

Ladle marinara sauce over the cutlets and arrange the mozzarella on top. Transfer skillet to oven and bake for 15–17 minutes, or until cheese is melted and bubbly and sauce is hot. Sprinkle with remaining Parmesan. Serve over pasta, in sandwiches, or on its own. Makes 4 servings.

TOFU SANDWICHES

The following sandwich recipes each use one recipe of Tofu Filets on page 74, in addition to the ingredients listed for each sandwich. Use 2 filets for each serving, making 4 sandwiches total for each recipe.

Reuben Style Sandwiches:

I cup	**sauerkraut,** drained
4 tablespoons	**Thousand Island dressing**
8 slices	**dark rye bread**
4 slices	**Swiss cheese**

Heat sauerkraut in microwave for 60 seconds; drain thoroughly. Spread dressing on bread. Spread sauerkraut on 4 slices of bread and top with Swiss cheese. Place warm Tofu Filets on top of cheese and then top with remaining bread slices.

TLTs:

I	**large ripe tomatoe,** sliced
4	**lettuce leaves**
4 tablespoons	**Tofu Mayonnaise** (see Sauces, Dressings and Spreads, page 24)
8 slices	**lightly toasted and buttered bread**

Layer all ingredients on bread slices and top with warm Tofu Filets.

Grilled Veggie Style:

I	**large yellow onion,** sliced
2 cups	**sliced mushrooms**
2 tablespoons	**butter**
I teaspoon	**garlic salt**
4	**large buns,** lightly toasted
4 tablespoons	**Tofu Mayonnaise**
	(see Sauces, Dressings and Spreads, page 24) **and/or mustard**

Saute onion and mushrooms in butter until the onion begins to brown and the mushrooms are softened and the liquid evaporates; add garlic salt. Spread buns with Tofu Mayonnaise and/or mustard, and top with grilled veggies and warm Tofu Filets.

CHICKEN-FRIED TOFU TRIANGLES

14 ounces **extra-firm tofu,** drained and pressed dry
$^1/_2$ cup **cocktail sauce**
2 tablespoons **soy sauce**
1 teaspoon **garlic powder**
$^1/_4$ cup **canola oil**
1 $^1/_2$ cups **crumb coating,** such as panko

Cut tofu in half width wise. Cut each half into three planks about $^1/_2$ inch thick. Cut each plank into 2 triangles. Mix cocktail sauce, soy sauce and garlic powder. Heat oil in a small saute pan until medium hot. Dip each triangle on all sides in sauce mixture. Spread crumb coating on a small plate and press triangles into coating. Place in pan and cook about 3 minutes on each side, or until well browned. Makes 4–6 servings.

CHEATBALLS

14 ounces	**extra-firm tofu,** drained and firmly pressed
1	**small onion,** finely chopped
1/2 cup	**finely chopped Italian pepper** (cubanelle)
3 cloves	**garlic,** minced
1/2 teaspoon each	**salt and pepper,** or to taste
1 teaspoon	**Italian seasoning**
1/4 cup	**chopped fresh basil**
1/4 teaspoon	**crushed red pepper**
2 cups	**marinara sauce,** divided
1 cup	**seasoned breadcrumbs**
2	**eggs or egg substitute**
1/4 cup	**grated Parmesan cheese** (optional)

Preheat oven to 425 degrees.

Combine first 8 ingredients plus 1 tablespoon marinara sauce and mix and squeeze by hand as with a meatloaf. Cover and refrigerate 1 hour. Add breadcrumbs, eggs and Parmesan (if using) and mix again. Roll into balls and place on an oiled baking dish. Bake 15 minutes and then turn the balls and bake 15 minutes more, or until golden brown. Heat remaining marinara sauce and pour over top. Serves 4 a la carte or 6 when served with pasta.

INTERNATIONAL ENTREES

THAI COCONUT CURRY

14 ounces	**firm tofu,** frozen and thawed
1	**medium yellow onion**
2 tablespoons	**peanut oil**
1 tablespoon	**grated ginger**
2 teaspoons	**crushed garlic**
1 cup	**vegetable broth**
1 can (6 ounces)	**coconut milk**
2 tablespoons	**red curry paste** (or another mild curry paste)
1/4 cup	**golden raisins**
1/2 cup	**unsweetened coconut flakes**
2 tablespoons	**mango chutney or apricot jam**

Cut tofu into approximately 1/2-inch cubes. Halve the onion and then cut into long, thin strips about 1/4 inch thick. Heat oil over medium heat in a large frying pan. Add onion, ginger and garlic, stirring to flavor the oil, about 1 minute. Add tofu and continue stirring another 4 minutes.

Pour in vegetable broth and then blend in coconut milk. Add curry paste, raisins and coconut. Bring to a boil and then reduce heat to low. Add chutney, stirring in thoroughly, allowing mixture to thicken; simmer 15 minutes. Serve over jasmine or brown rice. Garnish with chopped peanuts, if desired. Makes 6 servings.

TOFU TIKKA MASALA

Marinade:

1/4 cup	**plain yogurt**
I tablespoon	**grated fresh ginger**
I tablespoon	**crushed garlic**
1/2 teaspoon each	**turmeric, curry powder, nutmeg and chili powder**
juice of 1/2	**lemon**
2 tablespoons	**extra virgin olive oil**
28 ounces	**firm tofu,** frozen, thawed and pressed
2 tablespoons	**butter**

Sauce:

I	**medium onion,** diced
2 tablespoons	**extra virgin olive oil**
I can (26 ounces)	**crushed tomatoes,** with liquid
2 tablespoons	**garam masala powder**
1/2 cup	**heavy cream**
I tablespoon	**honey**

Whisk all marinade ingredients except tofu and butter together and pour half into a baking dish. Cut tofu into cubes about 1 1/2 inches thick, add to baking dish and cover with remaining marinade. Cover and chill 2–3 hours or overnight. Preheat oven to 375 degrees. Add butter to the pan and bake tofu in marinade for 30 minutes, basting every 10 minutes.

In a large saucepan over medium-heat, saute onion in oil until browned. Add tomatoes and garam masala; reduce heat to low. Simmer 15 minutes, stirring occasionally. Remove tofu from its marinade with slotted spoon and add to saucepan, discarding excess marinade. Stir in cream and honey. Serve over jasmine or saffron rice. Garnish with fresh cilantro, if desired. Makes 6–8 servings.

SPANAKOPITA TRIANGLES

2 cups	**chopped onion**
1/3 cup	**olive oil,** divided
3 cloves	**garlic,** chopped
20 ounces	**frozen chopped spinach,** thawed and drained
14 ounces	**firm tofu,** pressed
1 tablespoon	**lemon juice**
1/2 teaspoon	**nutmeg**
1 teaspoon each	**salt and fresh black pepper**
16 ounces	**phyllo dough,** thawed in refrigerator

Preheat oven to 375 degrees.

In a large frying pan, saute onion in 2 tablespoons olive oil over medium-high heat for 3–4 minutes, or until softened. Add garlic and spinach, reduce heat to low and cook 5 minutes more. Combine spinach, onion and garlic in a food processor with tofu, lemon juice, and spices. Pulse until smooth.

Unroll phyllo dough and take out half the sheets, refrigerating remaining sheets until needed. Cut each sheet into 3 lengthwise strips. Lay 2 strips at a time over wax paper and brush well with olive oil. Put 1 1/2 to 2 tablespoons spinach filling in one corner of each strip and fold into a triangle. Continue to fold strip over and over in to a triangle, flag-style. Brush finished triangle with oil again, sealing any remaining edges. Place on a lightly greased baking sheet. Repeat with remaining spinach mixture. Bake 18–20 minutes, or until golden. Makes 6–8 servings.

TOFU PICCATA

2 tablespoons	**olive oil,** divided
³/₄ cup	**dry white wine or white grape juice,** divided*
2 teaspoons	**sugar**
2 cloves	**garlic,** minced
¹/₃ cup	**white miso paste**
juice and zest of	**1 lemon**
14 ounces	**extra-firm tofu,** frozen, thawed and pressed
3 tablespoons	**flour**
1 tablespoon	**capers**

Preheat oven to 350 degrees.

Combine half the oil and ¹/₂ cup wine or white grape juice with sugar, garlic, miso, lemon juice and zest in a small saucepan. Bring to a boil and cook, stirring constantly, for 1 minute; set aside. Cut block of tofu lengthwise into 4 strips. Place in a small baking pan and pour sauce over the strips, turning once so the tofu is completely coated. Bake for 30 minutes. Remove from oven and let cool completely.

Remove cooled tofu strips from baking pan, reserving marinade and excess coating. Roll each piece in flour until evenly coated. Heat remaining oil in a nonstick pan over medium heat. Add tofu and cook, turning once, until golden brown on each side; remove tofu. Add the reserved marinade, remaining vinegar and capers to the pan. Bring to a boil and cook 1–2 minutes, or until sauce is thickened. Pour over tofu and serve with pasta or vegetables. Makes 4 servings.

*If using white grape juice, omit sugar.

SWEET & SOUR SOY

I can (20 ounces)	**pineapple chunks,** reserving juice
juice and zest of I	**orange**
2 tablespoons each	**minced garlic and ginger**
2 tablespoons	**soy sauce**
3 tablespoons	**rice vinegar**
2 tablespoons	**peanut oil**
I	**large onion,** chopped
I	**carrot,** julienned or shredded
14 ounces	**extra-firm tofu,** drained, pressed and cubed
I each	**red and green bell pepper,** chopped
4 tablespoons	**cornstarch**
I cup	**whole salted cashews**

Drain pineapple juice into a saucepan and set pineapple chunks aside. Add orange juice and zest, garlic, ginger, soy sauce and vinegar and whisk together over medium-high heat. Reduce heat, cover and let simmer. Heat oil in a wok or large frying pan. Add onion and cook on high for 2 minutes. Add carrot and cook 4 minutes more, stirring continuously. Add tofu and bell peppers and then cook for about 4 minutes more, still stirring constantly; reduce heat.

In a small bowl, whisk together cornstarch and $1/4$ cup of the seasoning sauce, just until cornstarch is thoroughly dissolved. Add mixture to saucepan and stir as it thickens. Pour thickened sauce into the wok or skillet, turning heat up to high. Add reserved pineapple chunks and cashews. Combine all ingredients until the pineapple is hot and everything is coated with sauce. Serve over rice. Makes 4 servings.

TOFU FRIED RICE

Sauce:

1/3 cup	**vegetable broth**
1/8 cup	**soy sauce**
2 teaspoons	**sugar**
2 teaspoons	**toasted sesame oil**

Rice:

5 tablespoons	**peanut oil,** divided
14 ounces	**firm tofu,** drained, pressed and cut into 1/2-inch cubes
1/2	**small onion,** grated
2 tablespoons	**gingerroot,** grated or minced
2 cloves	**garlic,** minced
1	**red bell pepper,** finely chopped
4	**whole scallions,** thinly sliced on an angle
6 cups	**cooked rice,** chilled
2 cups	**bean sprouts**

Whisk all sauce ingredients together and then set aside. In a wok or large saute pan, heat 2 tablespoons peanut oil. Add tofu cubes and stir-fry on high heat until lightly golden. Remove tofu with a slotted spoon, and set on paper towels to drain.

Add remaining oil to pan and heat again. Add onion, ginger, garlic and bell pepper, stir-fry about 1 minute. Add the scallions and continue stir-frying another minute. Add tofu, rice and sprouts. Pour in sauce. Stir all ingredients together until well combined and the rice has been reheated. Season with salt and pepper to taste. Serve with a little extra sesame oil drizzled over top, if desired. Makes 6–8 servings.

STROMBOLI ROLL

1/4 cup	**olive oil,** divided
1 large	**onion,** chopped
1 cup	**broccoli florets,** chopped
1	**yellow bell pepper,** thinly sliced
3 cloves	**garlic,** minced
14 ounces	**extra-firm tofu,** drained and crumbled
1 can (14 ounces)	**diced tomatoes,** drained
1 teaspoon each	**dried basil and oregano**
1/2 teaspoon	**crushed red pepper flakes**
1 ball (about 16 ounces)	**uncooked pizza dough**
	marinara sauce (optional)

Preheat oven to 400 degrees.

Heat 2 tablespoons oil in a large frying pan. Add onion and cook over medium heat about 4–5 minutes, or until softened. Add broccoli, bell pepper and garlic. Cover and cook 5 minutes more. Stir in tofu, tomatoes and spices. Lower heat to medium-low and cook about 10 minutes, stirring occasionally, or until all liquid has evaporated.

Roll out the pizza dough into a 9 x 12-inch rectangle on a floured sheet of wax paper. Spread with the filling, leaving about an inch around the edge of the dough. Roll lengthwise into a long log. Invert onto a large baking sheet seam side down and brush the roll with the remaining oil. Bake for 35–40 minutes, or until dough is golden brown. Slice crosswise to serve and top with marinara sauce, if desired. Makes 6 servings.

VEGAN PALAK PANEER

14 ounces	**firm tofu,** diced into ¹/₂-inch cubes
2 tablespoons	**canola oil**
¹/₂ cup	**chopped onion**
1 inch	**ginger,** chopped
3 cloves	**garlic,** chopped
1	**jalapeno pepper,** chopped
1 teaspoon	**cumin**
1 dash each	**nutmeg and cayenne pepper**
1 cup	**water**
10 ounces	**frozen chopped spinach,** thawed and squeezed dry
6 ounces	**soy yogurt**

Bring about 4 cups salted water to a boil in a small saucepan. Add the tofu and reduce heat to low; simmer for 4 minutes and then drain and set aside. Heat oil in a nonstick pan and add the onion, ginger, garlic and jalapeno; saute for 5 minutes. Add spices and water and let simmer 5 minutes more. Transfer mixture to a food processor, add spinach and then puree. Return pureed mixture to the pan and stir in yogurt, simmering again for 3–4 minutes, or until heated through. Serve over rice. Makes 4–6 servings.

VEGETARIAN PAELLA

2 tablespoons	**olive oil**
1 1/2 tablespoons	**butter or margarine**
1	**large onion,** chopped
2 cups	**arborio (risotto) rice**
1/2 teaspoon	**saffron threads,** crumbled
14 ounces	**extra-firm tofu,** drained, pressed and cubed
1/4 cup	**white wine or white wine vinegar**
1 each	**red and green bell pepper,** diced
1/2 cup each	**celery and carrot,** diced
3 cloves	**garlic,** minced
8 ounces	**tempeh,** cubed
8 ounces	**seitan,** sliced
5 cups	**vegetable broth**
1 cup	**frozen peas**

Preheat oven to 350 degrees.

Heat oil and butter over medium-high heat in a very large frying pan (cast iron is preferable) or Dutch oven. Add onion and saute until it begins to soften, about 3 minutes. Add rice and stir until coated with the butter and oil. Sprinkle saffron into the pan and stir until coloring is evenly distributed. Add tofu and then pour in white wine vinegar.

Reduce heat to medium and stir mixture continuously until absorbed and evaporated. Stir in remaining ingredients except broth and peas. Add vegetable broth 1 cup at a time, stirring until each cup is absorbed (more stock may be added if mixture starts to dry out). Stir in peas. Cover pot and let simmer until rice is tender and has absorbed all liquid, about 15 minutes. Makes 6–8 servings.

BLACK BEAN ENCHILADAS

14	**corn tortillas**
3 tablespoons	**butter**
1 can (15 ounces)	**black beans,** rinsed and drained
14 ounces	**extra-firm tofu,** rinsed and drained
2 teaspoons	**chili powder**
4 cups	**finely grated sharp cheddar cheese,** divided
1 can (28 ounces)	**red enchilada sauce**

Preheat oven to 350 degrees.

Saute each tortilla over medium-high heat in a little butter until lightly crisp but still bendable, about 30 seconds on each side. Mash black beans in a small mixing bowl. Add tofu and mash. Stir in chili powder and 3 cups cheese. Spread a thin layer of enchilada sauce in a 9 x 13-inch baking pan. Roll $^1/_4$ cup bean mixture in each tortilla and place in pan. When pan is filled, pour remaining enchilada sauce over top. Bake 30–40 minutes, or until cooked through and bubbly. Remove from oven and sprinkle remaining cheese over top. Makes 6–8 servings.

VARIATION: Substitute a can of whole pinto beans for the can of black beans. Add 1 can (4 ounces) diced green chiles into bean mixture. Substitute Monterey Jack cheese for cheddar cheese and green enchilada sauce for red enchilada sauce.

TOFU CACCIATORE

3 tablespoons	**olive oil**
1	**large onion,** chopped
4 cloves	**garlic,** minced
8 ounces	**mushrooms,** sliced
28 ounces	**extra-firm tofu,** drained, pressed and cut into strips
2 tablespoons	**flour**
$^1/_2$ cup	**red wine vinegar**
$^1/_2$ cup	**vegetable broth**
1 can (15 ounces)	**diced tomatoes,** drained
1 $^1/_2$ teaspoons	**Italian seasoning**
$^1/_2$ cup	**grated Parmesan cheese**
	salt and pepper

Preheat oven to 350 degrees.

Heat oil in a large frying pan. Add onion and saute 2 minutes over medium-high heat. Add garlic, mushrooms and tofu to pan. Continue sauteing another 5–6 minutes, or until onions have softened and ingredients are well combined. Add flour and continue cooking mixture, stirring continuously, another 3 minutes. Add vinegar, broth, tomatoes and seasoning. Transfer mixture to a casserole dish coated with non-stick spray. Sprinkle Parmesan cheese over top and bake 30 minutes. Season with salt and pepper to taste. Makes 6 servings.

VEGETARIAN PAD THAI

12 ounces	**rice (pad thai) noodles**
4 tablespoons	**peanut oil,** divided
14 ounces	**extra-firm tofu,** drained, pressed and cut into $1/2$-inch cubes
2 tablespoons	**soy sauce**
1	**red bell pepper,** julienned
2 cloves	**garlic,** minced
6	**scallions,** finely chopped
2 tablespoons	**brown sugar**
3 tablespoons	**rice vinegar**
$1/2$ cup	**chopped peanuts**
$1/2$ cup	**bean sprouts**
	crushed red pepper flakes, to taste

Boil rice noodles according to package directions. Drain and toss with 1 tablespoon oil; set aside. Heat another tablespoon oil in large frying pan over medium-high and add tofu cubes and soy sauce. Saute for 4 minutes, or until light brown. Remove from pan and set aside. Add remaining oil to pan. Saute bell pepper, garlic and scallions for 5 minutes. Add brown sugar and rice vinegar and cook for 2 minutes, stirring occasionally. Add rice noodles and tofu back to the pan and stir all ingredients together, cooking until noodles and tofu are combined and heated. Toss in peanuts, bean sprouts and crushed red pepper flakes. Makes 4–6 servings.

DESSERTS

TRIPLEBERRY TARTS

14 ounces	**firm tofu,** drained
$^1/_2$ cup	**lemon curd**
3 tablespoons	**powdered sugar**
1 teaspoon	**vanilla**
12	**mini graham cracker or regular individual piecrusts**
3 cups	**berries,** any combination
1 container (6 ounces)	**frozen limeade concentrate,** thawed
2 tablespoons	**cornstarch**
$^1/_4$ cup	**sugar**

In a food processor or blender, mix tofu, lemon curd, powdered sugar and vanilla. Place 3 tablespoons tofu mixture in tart crusts. Chop berries so that they are uniform in size, about the size of a peanut. Spread 4 tablespoons mixed berries on top in tart crusts.

In a small saucepan, bring limeade, cornstarch and sugar to a boil. Cook on high heat, stirring constantly, for 2–3 minutes, or until thickened. Remove from heat and let cool a few minutes. Brush glaze generously on top of berries, using all the glaze. Refrigerate at least 1 hour, or overnight. Makes 12 tarts.

REBIRTH BY CHOCOLATE

14 ounces	**firm tofu,** drained
2 tablespoons	**powdered sugar**
2 teaspoons	**vanilla**
1/2 cup	**milk**
1 bag (12 ounces)	**semisweet chocolate chips,** melted
2 cups	**crushed chocolate cookie crumbs**
1/4 cup	**butter,** melted
	whipped topping
	shaved dark chocolate

In a food processor or high-speed blender, blend tofu, powdered sugar, vanilla and milk. Stir chocolate chips into tofu mixture. If using a blender, this may take several cycles of re-stirring the mixture, packing it down and blending again; repeat the process until smooth. Mix cookie crumbs and butter together and then press into the bottom and 1 inch up the sides of a springform pan. Pour tofu mixture on top and spread until even. Refrigerate 1 hour or until well chilled. Cut into pieces and then garnish on a plate with whipped topping and shaved chocolate. Makes 6–8 servings.

VARIATION: Use a ready-made chocolate crust for convenience in place of cookie crumbs and butter.

VEGAN VARIATION: Use vanilla soy milk in place of milk and margarine (or another non-dairy spread) in place of butter.

CAFE MOCHA VARIATION: Use milk chocolate in place of semisweet and add 3–4 teaspoons dissolved instant coffee into blender mixture. Sprinkle an additional teaspoon of instant coffee over the whipped topping in place of shaved chocolate.

RASPBERRY CHOCOLATE CHUNK PIE

14 ounces	**firm tofu,** drained and pressed
1/2 teaspoon	**almond extract**
1/2 cup	**raspberry jam or preserves,** divided
2 tablespoons	**powdered sugar,** divided
1 bag (12 ounces)	**milk chocolate chips,** melted
1 dozen	**plain chocolate wafer cookies**
1	**graham cracker crust**

Break the tofu into small chunks and put in a blender. Add almond extract, 1/4 cup jam, and 1 tablespoon powdered sugar and then fold in melted chocolate. Puree in a food processor or high-speed blender. If using a blender, this may take several cycles of re-stirring the mixture, packing it down and blending again; repeat the process until smooth. Crumble cookies into small pieces (not too fine) and stir into mixture, then pour into graham cracker crust.

Combine remaining jam and powdered sugar and then heat in microwave for 30 seconds. Pour the jam mixture in a single spiral line over the top of the pie, then take a knife and zigzag across the spiral. Chill for at least 1 hour. Makes 6–8 servings.

GOOEY SPICE BARS

1 box (18 ounces)	**spice cake mix**
1/2 cup	**margarine or other non-dairy spread,** softened
6 ounces	**silken tofu,** divided
1/2 cup	**chopped nuts**
3 3/4 cups	**powdered sugar**
8 ounces	**soft tofu**
1 teaspoon	**vanilla**
2 tablespoons each	**cinnamon and sugar,** combined

Preheat oven to 350 degrees.

Mix cake mix, margarine and one-third of the silken tofu. Spread mixture into a greased 9 x 13-inch pan. Sprinkle nuts over top. In a blender or food processor, combine powdered sugar, remaining silken tofu, soft tofu and vanilla. Blend on high until smooth. Pour over cake mixture and nuts in pan. Bake 35–40 minutes, or until the top layer turns golden brown and bubbly. Sprinkle cinnamon sugar over top as it cools. Cut into bars. Makes 12 servings.

VARIATION: Use carrot cake mix instead of spice cake mix and add 1/2 cup raisins to cake batter before baking. Stir 1/2 cup coconut flakes into the powdered sugar and tofu mixture after blending.

PEANUT BUTTER CUP

I cup	**creamy peanut butter**
14 ounces	**firm tofu,** drained, pressed and divided
4 tablespoons	**powdered sugar,** divided
2 teaspoons	**vanilla extract,** divided
I	**chocolate cookie crust**
I bag (6 ounces)	**semisweet chocolate chips**
	chopped nuts

Combine peanut butter, half the tofu, 2 tablespoons powdered sugar and I teaspoon vanilla extract in a food processor or high-speed blender. Puree on high until smooth. When smooth, pour and spread into bottom of cookie crust. Melt chocolate in a double boiler. Combine the remaining tofu with the remaining sugar and vanilla in the blender and then fold in chocolate and blend on high until smooth. Pour over the peanut butter mixture, covering it completely. Sprinkle nuts over top. Makes 6–8 servings.

VARIATION: In addition to a sprinkling of nuts, top it off by heating an additional 2–3 tablespoons peanut butter with I teaspoon powdered sugar and pour in a spiral over the top. Then, using a knife, draw a zigzag line through the spiral. Chill for at least I hour.

CREAMY COOKIE PIE

14 ounces	**firm tofu,** drained and pressed
1 teaspoon	**vanilla extract**
1/4 cup	**powdered sugar**
1 bag (12 ounces)	**white chocolate chips,** melted
20	**chocolate wafer cookies**
1	**chocolate cookie crust**

Break tofu into small chunks and put in a food processor or high-speed blender. Add vanilla and powdered sugar and blend in a food processor or high speed blender. Once the mixture is well combined but not yet smooth, pour the melted chocolate in and stir. Puree on high speed. If using a blender, this may take several cycles of re-stirring the mixture, packing it down and blending again; repeat the process until smooth.

Crumble the cookies into small pieces. Handful by handful, stir cookie pieces into the mixture, reserving the smallest pieces and crumbs for sprinkling over the top. Pour into chocolate crust and top with the left-over crumbs. Chill for at least 1 hour. Makes 6–8 servings.

RASPBERRY DELIGHT

¹/₂ cup	**butter or margarine**
I cup	**white or whole wheat flour**
¹/₄ cup	**brown sugar**
¹/₂ cup	**chopped walnuts**
8 ounces	**firm tofu,** drained
I container (8 ounces)	**frozen whipped topping,** thawed
I teaspoon	**vanilla**
I cup	**powdered sugar**
I ¹/₂ cups	**water**
I box (4.75 ounces)	**Danish Dessert**
2 cups	**fresh or frozen raspberries**

Cut butter into flour and then mix with brown sugar and nuts.
Spread in a 9 x 13-inch pan and bake at 375 degrees for 15 minutes,
stirring every 5 minutes. Remove from oven and cool. Process tofu,
whipped topping, vanilla and powdered sugar at medium speed in a
food processor or high-speed blender for 3 minutes, or until fluffy.
Pour tofu mixture over crust. Bring water to a boil and add Danish
Dessert, stirring until clear and thickened. Remove from heat and
add raspberries. Pour over tofu mixture and chill until set. Makes
12 servings.

TOFU PUMPKIN PIE

1 can (28 ounces)	**pumpkin**
1 1/4 cups	**dark brown sugar**
1 teaspoon	**salt**
2 teaspoons	**cinnamon**
1/2 teaspoon each	**ground ginger, cloves and nutmeg**
14 ounces	**firm tofu,** drained
2	**unbaked 9-inch pie shells**

Preheat oven to 425 degrees.

Blend all ingredients together except pie shells in a food processor or blender until well blended, about 1 minute. Pour into pie shells and bake for 15 minutes. Reduce heat to 350 degrees and bake 45 minutes more. Chill and serve. Makes 2 pies with 6–8 servings each.

DAIRY-FREE CHOCOLATE PUDDING

16 ounces	**silken tofu**
1/2 cup	**powdered sugar**
1 tablespoon	**vanilla**
1 bag (12 ounces)	**semisweet chocolate chips**

Process tofu in a food processor for about 1 minute. Add powdered sugar and vanilla and continue processing. Melt chocolate chips on low heat in a glass bowl in the microwave for about 3 minutes, stirring occasionally and checking to make sure chips are just melted and not burning. When melted, add a spoonful at a time to tofu mixture while processing. The mixture should be the consistency of sour cream. If necessary, add a little water. Refrigerate until chilled (mixture will thicken slightly while chilling) and then serve. Makes 6–8 servings.

VARIATION: Use butterscotch chips in place of chocolate chips.

CLASSIC CHEESEFAKE

1 1/2 cups	**plain or cinnamon graham cracker crumbs**
6 tablespoons	**butter or margarine,** melted
3 packages (8 ounces each)	**soy cream cheese,** softened
16 ounces	**silken tofu**
2 tablespoons	**lemon juice**
1/3 cup	**flour**
1 cup	**sugar**

Preheat oven to 350 degrees.

Mix graham cracker crumbs and butter together and then press into the bottom of a 9-inch springform pan; let chill in refrigerator.

In a food processor or high-speed blender, combine all remaining ingredients. Pour over crust and then place pan inside a large, deep baking dish. Fill the baking dish with hot water, taking care not to disturb the springform pan inside and transfer to the oven. Bake 50 minutes and then turn off the oven. Open the oven door, and let cheesecake sit for about 1 hour. Remove from oven and transfer springform pan to the refrigerator. Chill, covered, for at least 3 hours. Makes 6–8 servings.

CHOCOLATE CHEESEFAKE

1 1/2 cups	**chocolate graham cracker crumbs**
6 tablespoons	**butter or margarine,** melted
2 packages (8 ounces each)	**soy cream cheese,** softened
16 ounces	**silken tofu**
1 bag (16 ounces)	**semisweet chocolate chips,** melted
1/3 cup	**flour**
1 cup	**sugar**

Preheat oven to 350 degrees.

Mix graham cracker crumbs and butter together and then press into the bottom of a 9-inch springform pan; let chill in refrigerator.

In a food processor or high-speed blender, combine all remaining ingredients. Pour over crust and then place pan inside a large, deep baking dish. Fill the baking dish with hot water, taking care not to disturb the springform pan inside and transfer to the oven. Bake 50 minutes and then turn off the oven. Open the oven door and let cheesecake sit for about 1 hour. Remove from oven and transfer springform pan to the refrigerator. Chill, covered, for at least 3 hours. Makes 6–8 servings.

LEMON CUSTARD CUPS

14 ounces	**firm tofu,** drained and pressed
1 can (15 ounces)	**lemon pie filling**
1/4 cup	**powdered sugar**
4 tablespoons	**Rose's Lime Juice or frozen limeade concentrate**
12	**mini graham cracker crusts**

In a food processor or high-speed blender, puree first four ingredients on high until smooth. Pour into individual piecrusts and chill overnight. Makes 12 servings.

VARIATION: Sprinkle the top of each custard cup with lemon zest and/or raw sugar crystals.

COCONUT ALMOND BARS

1 1/2 cups	**chocolate wafer cookie crumbs**
6 tablespoons	**butter or margarine,** melted
14 ounces	**firm tofu,** drained, pressed and divided
1 bag (6 ounces)	**white chocolate chips,** melted
1 bag (12 ounces)	**shredded coconut**
1/2 cup	**sliced almonds**
1 tablespoon	**powdered sugar**
1 bag (12 ounces)	**dark or semisweet chocolate chips,** melted
1 teaspoon	**almond extract**
1/2 cup	**slivered almonds**

Mix cookie crumbs and butter together and then press into the bottom of a square pan and let chill in refrigerator.

In a food processor or high-speed blender, puree half the tofu with the white chocolate at high speed until smooth. Stir in coconut, sliced almonds and powdered sugar. Press over cookie crust.

Blend the melted dark chocolate with the remaining tofu and the almond extract. Stir in the slivered almonds. Pour over the coconut mixture and garnish as desired. Chill at least 1 hour, cut into squares. Makes 12 servings.

VARIATION: Garnish with whole roasted (but unsalted) almonds.

CREME BRULEE

16 ounces	**silken tofu**
1 tablespoon	**vanilla extract**
1/8 teaspoon	**nutmeg**
1/8 teaspoon	**salt**
2 tablespoons	**cornstarch**
1/2 cup plus 8 teaspoons	**sugar**

Preheat oven to 375 degrees.

Put all ingredients except 8 teaspoons sugar into a blender and puree until smooth. Pour into 4 ramekins and then arrange in a baking dish. Pour enough hot water into the baking dish to come halfway up the sides of the ramekins. Bake until the tops slightly brown and a knife inserted in the middle comes out clean, about 50–55 minutes. Remove ramekins from water bath and cool slightly. Chill at least 2–3 hours.

Gently spread 2 teaspoons sugar over the top of each custard, smoothing into an even surface. Caramelize the sugar with a culinary torch (following all manufacturer's instructions), moving the torch continuously over the surface in small circles and let the crust harden. Allow to cool before serving. Makes 4 servings.

TOFU ICE CREAM DESSERTS

French Silk Chocolate:

16 ounces	**silken tofu**
1/2 cup	**cocoa powder**
1 cup	**soy milk**
1 tablespoon	**vanilla**
1/4 cup	**canola oil**
1/2 teaspoon	**salt**
1 cup	**sugar**

Strawberry Banana:

16 ounces	**silken tofu**
1	**banana,** peeled
16 ounces	**strawberries,** stems removed
1 cup	**sugar**
1/2 cup	**soy milk**
1 tablespoon	**lemon juice**
1 tablespoon	**vanilla**
1/2 teaspoon	**salt**

ICE CREAM MAKER METHOD: Blend the ingredients for one of the above desserts in a food processor or blender. Freeze in ice cream maker following manufacturer's directions.

FREEZER AND FOOD PROCESSOR METHOD: Blend the ingredients for one of the above desserts in a food processor. Place one-third of the mixture in the refrigerator and two-thirds of mixture in the freezer. When the freezer mixture is frozen, remove and with a large sturdy knife cut into cubes. Place the refrigerated mixture in food processor and turn on. Slowly add frozen cubes one at a time. Blend until mixture is thick and creamy. Makes 4–6 servings.

LEMON RASPBERRY TIRAMISU

2	**eggs**
2	**egg yolks**
3/4 cup	**sugar**
16 ounces	**firm tofu,** drained
2 tablespoons	**vanilla**
1/2 cup	**lemon curd**
2 cups	**frozen raspberries,** thawed
24	**ladyfingers** (hard variety)

In a small saucepan, cook eggs, egg yolks and sugar for 3–5 minutes over medium heat, stirring constantly until thickened.

In a food processor or blender, blend egg mixture, tofu, vanilla and lemon curd until well blended. Drain liquid from thawed raspberries into a small bowl. Add water to make 2 cups total raspberry juice. Spray a 9 x 13-inch baking pan with nonstick cooking spray. Dip each ladyfinger in raspberry juice for 1 second on each side and then layer in pan to completely cover. Repeat this process for a second layer of ladyfingers. Discard remaining juice. Spread raspberries on top. Spread tofu mixture over raspberries. Cover and refrigerate 8 hours or overnight; serve cold. Makes 8–10 servings.

CLASSIC TIRAMISU VARIATION: Omit the lemon curd and raspberries. In place of raspberry juice, mix 1 cup coffee with 2 tablespoons sugar and 2 tablespoons chocolate syrup.

WORLD'S HEALTHIEST BROWNIES

1 1/3 cups	**regular or whole wheat flour**
1 teaspoon	**baking soda**
1 teaspoon	**cinnamon**
3/4 cup	**sugar**
1/2 cup	**cocoa powder**
1/4 cup	**applesauce**
1 tablespoon	**canola oil**
1 teaspoon	**vanilla**
16 ounces	**silken tofu**
1/2 cup	**chopped walnuts** (optional)

Preheat oven to 350 degrees.

Mix flour, baking soda, cinnamon, sugar and cocoa powder. In a blender, mix applesauce, oil, vanilla and tofu until well blended. Stir into dry ingredients. Stir in nuts if desired. Spray a 9 x 13-inch square baking pan with nonstick cooking spray. Pour in batter. Bake for 45–50 minutes, or until firm on top. Makes 16 snack-size squares.

DESSERT PIZZA

1 box (19 ounces)	**brownie mix**
2	**large eggs**
^{1}/$_3$ cup	**canola oil**
3 tablespoons	**water**
8 ounces	**silken tofu**
1 box (3.4 ounces)	**cheesecake or vanilla instant pudding mix**
1 cup	**frozen non-dairy whipped topping,** thawed
8 cups	**thinly sliced fruit**
	chocolate syrup

Preheat oven to 350 degrees.

Mix together brownie mix, eggs, oil and water until blended. Spray nonstick spray on a 15-inch round pizza pan with sides. Pour brownie mixture and spread evenly over pan. Bake 16–18 minutes, or until cooked through in center. Remove from oven and cool.

In a blender or food processor, mix the tofu and pudding mix until smooth; chill at least 10 minutes. Fold in whipped topping and spread over cooled brownie crust. Chill for about 1 hour. Layer the sliced fruit on top and drizzle on chocolate syrup as a garnish. Cut into wedges and serve. Makes 8 servings.

NOTES

METRIC CONVERSION CHART

Volume Measurements		Weight Measurements		Temperature Conversion	
U.S.	Metric	U.S.	Metric	Fahrenheit	Celsius
1 teaspoon	5 ml	$^{1}/_{2}$ ounce	15 g	250	120
1 tablespoon	15 ml	1 ounce	30 g	300	150
$^{1}/_{4}$ cup	60 ml	3 ounces	90 g	325	160
$^{1}/_{3}$ cup	75 ml	4 ounces	115 g	350	180
$^{1}/_{2}$ cup	125 ml	8 ounces	225 g	375	190
$^{2}/_{3}$ cup	150 ml	12 ounces	350 g	400	200
$^{3}/_{4}$ cup	175 ml	1 pound	450 g	425	220
1 cup	250 ml	$2^{1}/_{4}$ pounds	1 kg	450	230

 Check out these "101" favorites
for more tasty recipes:

Bacon	**More Ramen**
Beans	**More Slow Cooker**
Beer	**Pickle**
Bundt® Pan	**Pumpkin**
Cake Mix	**Ramen Noodles**
Canned Biscuits	**Rice**
Casserole	**Sheet Pan**
Chile Peppers	**Slow Cooker**
Dutch Oven	**Toaster Oven**
Grits	**Tortilla**
Instant Pot	**Tots**
More Bacon	

Each 128 pages, $9.99

Available at bookstores or
directly from GIBBS SMITH
1.800.835.4993
www.gibbs-smith.com

ABOUT THE AUTHORS

Donna Kelly, a food fanatic and recipe developer, is the author of several cookbooks including French Toast, Quesadillas, 101 Things to Do with a Tortilla, and 101 Things to Do with An Instant Pot®. She lives in Salt Lake City, Utah.

Anne Tegtmeier established Fan Fare Themed Catering in 2017. After reuniting with her birth mother Donna Kelly in 1999, Anne and Donna discovered common interests and co-authored 101 Things to Do with Tofu and Virgin Vegan: Everyday Recipes for Satisfying Your Appetite. Anne attended Boot Camp training at the Culinary Institute of America, appeared on the Food Network's Ultimate Recipe Showdown, and currently co-writes the food blog Apron Strings with Donna. She lives in Portland, Oregon.